hands-on science
An Inquiry Approach

Properties of Matter for Grades K–2

Senior Author

Jennifer Lawson

PORTAGE & MAIN PRESS

Winnipeg • Manitoba • Canada

© 2019 Jennifer Lawson

Pages of this publication designated as reproducible with the following icon ![icon] may be reproduced under licence from Access Copyright. All other pages may be reproduced only with the permission of Portage & Main Press, or as permitted by law.

All rights are otherwise reserved, and no part of this publication may be reproduced, stored in a retrieval system, or transmitted in any form or by any means—electronic, mechanical, photocopying, scanning, recording, or otherwise—except as specifically authorized.

Portage & Main Press gratefully acknowledges the financial support of the Province of Manitoba through the Department of Sports, Culture, and Heritage and the Manitoba Book Publishing Tax Credit, and the Government of Canada through the Canada Book Fund (CBF), for our publishing activities.

Hands-On Science: An Inquiry Approach
Properties of Matter for Grades K–2

ISBN: 978-1-55379-799-9
Printed and bound in Canada by Prolific Group

0 1 2 3 4 5 6 7 8 9 10

Download the image banks and reproducibles that accompany this book by going to the Portage & Main Press website at <www.portageandmainpress.com/product/HOSMATTERK2/>. Use the password **OBJECTSANDMATERIALS** to access this free download.

The publisher has made every effort to acknowledge all sources of photographs used in the image banks and to ensure the authenticity of all Indigenous resources. The publisher would be grateful if any errors or omissions were pointed out, so that they may be corrected.

A special thank-you to the following people for their generous contributions to this project:

Project Consultants:
Faye Brownlie
Kathleen Gregory

Science Consultant:
Rosalind Poon

Early Years Consultants:
Lisa Schwartz
Deidre Sagert

Indigenous Consultant:
Melanie Nelson, Stó:lō and In-SHUCK-ch

Makerspace Contributors:
Joan Badger
Todd Johnson

Curriculum Correlation Consultant:
Susan Atcheson

Book and Cover Design:
Relish New Brand Experience Inc.

Cover Photo:
Adobestock

Illustrations:
ArtPlus Ltd.
26 Projects
Jess Dixon

PORTAGE & MAIN PRESS
www.portageandmainpress.com
customerservice@portageandmainpress.com
1-800-667-9673
Winnipeg, Manitoba
Treaty 1 Territory and homeland of the Métis Nation

Contents

Introduction to *Hands-On Science* ... 5
About *Hands-On Science* ... 5
Format of *Hands-On Science* ... 5
The Multi-Age Approach ... 6
Inquiry and Science ... 6
The Goals of Science Education in British Columbia ... 6
Hands-On Science Principles ... 7
Cultural Connections ... 8
Indigenous Perspectives and Knowledge ... 9
References ... 12

How to Use *Hands-On Science* in Your Classroom ... 13
Multi-Age Teaching and Learning ... 13
Module Overview ... 13
Talking Circles ... 16
Multiple Intelligences Learning Centres ... 17
Icons ... 18
Makerspace Centres ... 19
Loose Parts ... 20
References ... 21

Curricular Competencies: How to Infuse Scientific Inquiry Skills and Processes Into Lessons ... 22
Observing ... 22
Questioning ... 22
Exploring ... 22
Classifying ... 23
Measuring ... 23
Communicating, Analyzing, and Interpreting ... 24
Predicting ... 25
Inferring ... 25
Inquiry Through Investigation and Experimentation ... 25
Inquiry Through Research ... 26
Addressing Students' Early Literacy Needs ... 27
Online Considerations ... 27
References ... 28

The *Hands-On Science* Assessment Plan ... 29
Student Self-Assessment ... 29
Formative Assessment ... 31
Summative Assessment ... 32
Indigenous Perspectives on Assessment ... 33
Connecting Assessment to Curricular Competencies ... 33
Module Assessment Summary ... 34
Important Note to Teachers ... 34
References ... 34
Assessment Reproducibles ... 35

What Are the Properties of Matter? ... 59
About This Module ... 60
Curriculum Learning Framework ... 64
Curricular Competencies Correlation Chart ... 65
Resources for Students ... 67

1 Initiating Event: What Do We Observe, Think, and Wonder About Objects and Materials in Nature? ... 71
2 What Can We Learn About Objects and Materials Through Storytelling? ... 77
3 What Do We Know About Objects and Materials? ... 82
4 How Can We Describe Objects and Materials? ... 88
5 How Can We Sort Objects and Materials? ... 92
6 Why Are Some Materials Better Than Others for Certain Jobs? ... 96
7 How Can Different Materials Be Used to Construct Objects? ... 102

8 How Do We Decide Which Materials Are Best to Do a Job?	**106**
9 Why Is It Important to Choose the Right Material for the Job?	**111**
10 How Can We Change the Properties of Waste Materials to Use Them in Different Ways?	**116**
11 How Can We Use Materials in Different Ways to Design and Construct Objects?	**121**
12 What Do We Know About Solids and Liquids?	**125**
13 What Are Solids and Liquids?	**129**
14 What Are Some Properties of Liquids?	**135**
15 Can Liquids and Solids Be Mixed Together?	**142**
16 How Can We Combine Solids and Liquids to Make Useful Products?	**148**
17 What Are the Properties of Air?	**153**
18 What Is a Physical Change?	**158**
19 What Is a Chemical Change?	**162**
20 How Does Food Preparation Depend on Physical and Chemical Changes?	**167**
21 Inquiry Project: What More Do We Want to Know About the Properties of Matter?	**172**

Appendix: Image Banks 175

About the Contributors 180

***Hands-On Science* Order Form** 181

Introduction to *Hands-On Science*

About *Hands-On Science*

Hands-On Science helps develop students' scientific literacy through active inquiry, problem solving, and decision making. With each activity in *Hands-On Science*, students are encouraged to explore, investigate, and ask questions as a means of heightening their own curiosity about the world around them. Students solve problems through firsthand experiences and by observing and examining objects within their environment. In order for young students to develop scientific literacy, concrete experience is of utmost importance—in fact, it is essential.

Format of *Hands-On Science*

The redesigned Science Curriculum for British Columbia (<https://curriculum.gov.bc.ca/>) is based on a **"Know-Do-Understand"** model. The three elements—Content (Know), Curricular Competencies (Do), and Big Ideas (Understand) all work together to support deeper learning. *Hands-On Science* promotes this model through its inquiry-based, student-centred approach. As such, it is structured around the following elements.

The **Big Ideas** are broad concepts introduced in kindergarten and expanded upon in subsequent grades, fostering a deep understanding of science. The Big Ideas form the basis of the *Hands-On Science* modules to address important concepts in biology, chemistry, physics, and earth/space science.

The **Core Competencies** are embedded throughout the curriculum and throughout *Hands-On Science*. These competencies enable students to engage in deeper lifelong learning.

Core Competencies

Thinking	■ knowledge, skills, and processes that enable students to explore problems, weigh alternatives, and arrive at solutions ■ problem solving and making effective decisions, and applying them to real-world contexts
Communication	■ effectively reading, writing, speaking, listening, viewing, and representing ■ using a variety of information sources and digital tools
Personal and Social	■ relates to a student's identity as an individual and as a member of a group or community ■ contributing to the care of themselves, others, and the larger community

The **Learning Standards** are made up of **Curricular Competencies** and **Content**. **Curricular Competencies** are skills, strategies, and processes students develop as they explore science through hands-on activities. Curricular Competencies are addressed further on page 33.

The **Content** of the Science Curriculum for British Columbia and *Hands-On Science* is concept-based and relates directly to the Big Ideas. The Content relies on cross-cutting concepts developed throughout the grade levels, including:

- cause and effect
- change
- cycles
- evolution
- form and function
- interactions
- matter and energy
- order
- patterns
- systems

The Multi-Age Approach

Hands-On Science is designed with a multi-age approach to meet the needs of students in kindergarten to grade two (K–2). Each module explores the Big Ideas, Core Competencies, and Learning Standards for K–2. This approach provides teachers and students with flexible, personalized learning opportunities.

Inquiry and Science

Throughout *Hands-On Science*, as students explore science concepts, they are encouraged to ask questions to guide their own learning. The inquiry model is based on five components:

1. formulating questions
2. gathering and organizing information, evidence, or data
3. interpreting and analyzing information, evidence, or data
4. evaluating information, evidence, or data, and drawing conclusions
5. communicating findings

Using this model, teachers facilitate the learning, and students drive the process through inquiry. As such, the approach focuses on students' self-reflections as they ask questions, discover answers, and communicate their understanding. An inquiry approach begins with structured inquiry, moves to guided inquiry and, finally, results in open inquiry.

Structured Inquiry	■ The teacher provides the initial question and structures the procedures to answer it. ■ Students follow the given procedures and draw conclusions to answer the given question.
Guided Inquiry	■ The teacher provides the initial question. ■ Students are involved in designing ways to answer the question and communicate their findings.
Open Inquiry	■ Students formulate their own question(s), design and follow through with a developed procedure, and communicate their findings and results.

Inquiry takes time to foster and requires scaffolding from a structured approach to more open inquiry as students gain skills and experience.

In *Hands-On Science*, the focus of most activities is on guided inquiry, as teachers pose the main question for the lesson, based on the Learning Standards. Students are involved in generating further inquiry questions to personalize learning, but will continue to benefit from guidance and support from the teacher.

> Open inquiry activities are only successful if students are motivated by intrinsic interests and if they are equipped with the skills to conduct their own research study. (Banchi and Bell, 2008)

The Goals of Science Education in British Columbia

Science plays a fundamental role in the lives of Canadians. The Science Curriculum for British Columbia (<https://curriculum.gov.bc.ca/>) states:

> Science provides opportunities for us to better understand our natural world. Through science, we ask questions and seek answers to grow our collective scientific knowledge. We continually revise and refine our knowledge as we acquire new evidence. While maintaining our respect for evidence, we are aware that our scientific knowledge is provisional and is influenced by our culture, values, and ethics. Linking traditional and contemporary First Peoples understandings and current scientific knowledge enables us to make meaningful connections to our everyday lives and the world beyond.

> The Science curriculum takes a place-based approach to science learning. Students will develop place-based knowledge about the area in which they live, learning about and building on First Peoples knowledge and other traditional knowledge of the area. This provides a basis for an intuitive relationship with and respect for the natural world; connections to their ecosystem

and community; and a sense of relatedness that encourages lifelong harmony with nature.

The Science Curriculum for British Columbia identifies five goals that form the foundation of science education. In keeping with this focus on scientific literacy, these goals are the bases for the lessons in **Hands-On Science**. The Science Curriculum for British Columbia contributes to students' development as educated citizens through the achievement of the following goals. Students are expected to develop:

1. an understanding and appreciation of the nature of science as an evidence-based way of knowing the natural world that yields descriptions and explanations that are continually being improved within the context of our cultural values and ethics
2. place-based knowledge of the natural world and experience in the local area in which they live by accessing and building on existing understandings, including those of First Peoples
3. a solid foundation of conceptual and procedural knowledge in science that they can use to interpret the natural world and apply to new problems, issues, and events; to further learning; and to their lives
4. the habits of mind associated with science—a sustained curiosity; an appreciation for questions; an openness to new ideas and consideration of alternatives; an appreciation of evidence; an awareness of assumptions and a questioning of given information; a healthy, informed skepticism; a seeking of patterns, connections, and understanding; and a consideration of social, ethical, and environmental implications
5. a lifelong interest in science and the attitudes that will make them scientifically literate citizens who bring a scientific perspective, as appropriate, to social, moral, and ethical decisions and actions in their own lives, culture, and the environment

Hands-On Science Principles

- Effective science education involves hands-on inquiry, problem solving, and decision making.
- The development of Big Ideas, Core Competencies, Curricular Competencies, and Content form the foundation of science education.
- Children have a natural curiosity about science and the world around them. This curiosity must be maintained, fostered, and enhanced through active learning.
- Science activities must be meaningful, worthwhile, and related to real-life experiences.
- The teacher's role is to facilitate activities and encourage critical thinking and reflection. Children learn best by doing, rather than by just listening. Instead of simply telling, the teacher, therefore, should focus on formulating and asking questions, setting the conditions for students to ask their own questions, and helping students to make sense of the events and phenomena they have experienced.
- Science should be taught in conjunction with other school subjects. Themes and topics of study should integrate ideas and skills from several core areas whenever possible.
- Science education should encompass, and draw on, a wide range of educational resources, including literature, nonfiction research material, audio-visual resources, and technology, as well as people and places in the local community.
- Science education should be infused with knowledge and worldviews of Indigenous peoples, as well as other diverse multicultural perspectives.

- Science education should emphasize personalized learning. Personalized learning also focuses on enhancing student engagement and providing them with choices to explore and investigate ideas. Personalized learning also encompasses place-based learning, where learning focuses on the local environment.
- Science education is inclusive in nature. Learning opportunities should meet the diverse needs of all students through differentiated instruction and individualized learning experiences.
- Self-assessment is an integral part of science education. Students should be involved in reflecting on their work and setting new goals based on their reflections which, in turn, enables them to take control of their learning.
- Teacher assessment of student learning in science should be designed to focus on performance and understanding and should be conducted through meaningful assessment techniques implemented throughout each module.

Cultural Connections

To acknowledge and celebrate the cultural diversity represented in Canadian classrooms, it is important to infuse cultural connections into classroom learning experiences. It is essential for teachers to be aware of the cultural makeup of their class and to celebrate these diverse cultures by making connections to curricular outcomes. In the same way, it is important to explore other cultures represented in the community and beyond, to encourage intercultural understanding and harmony. For example, teachers in British Columbia should make connections to the local cultural communities to highlight their contributions to the province. Throughout *Hands-On Science*, suggestions are made for connecting science topics to cultural explorations and activities.

Indigenous Perspectives and Knowledge

Indigenous peoples are central to the Canadian context, and it is important to infuse Indigenous knowledge into the learning experiences of all students. The intentional integration of Indigenous knowledge in *Hands-On Science* helps to address the Calls to Action of the Truth and Reconciliation Commission of Canada, particularly the call to "integrate Indigenous knowledge and teaching methods into classrooms" (Action 62) and "build student capacity for intercultural understanding, empathy and mutual respect" (Action 63).

Indigenous peoples have depended on the land since time immemorial. The environment shapes the way of life: geography, vegetation, climate, and natural resources of the land determine the methods used to survive. Because they observe the land and its inhabitants, the environment teaches Indigenous peoples to survive. The land continues to shape Indigenous peoples' way of life today because of their ongoing, deep connection with the land. Cultural practices, stories, languages, and knowledge originate from the land.

The traditional territories of the First Peoples cover the entirety of what is now British Columbia. The worldviews of Indigenous peoples and their approaches and contributions to science are now being acknowledged and incorporated into science education. It is also important to recognize the diversity of Indigenous peoples in British Columbia and to focus on both the traditions and contemporary lives of the Indigenous communities in your area. Contact personnel in your school district—Indigenous consultants and/or those responsible for Indigenous education—to find out what resources (e.g., people, books, videos) are available. Many such resources are also featured in *Hands-On Science*.

NOTE: When implementing place-based learning, opportunities abound to consider Indigenous perspectives and knowledge. Outdoor learning provides an excellent opportunity to identify the importance of place. For example, use a map of the local area to have students identify where the location is in relation to the school. This will help students develop a stronger image of their community and surrounding area.

It is also important to identify on whose traditional territory the school is located, as well as the traditional territory of the location for the place-based learning. The following map, "First Nations in British Columbia," from Indigenous Services Canada can be used for this purpose: <https://www.aadnc-aandc.gc.ca/DAM/DAM-INTER-BC/STAGING/texte-text/fnmp_1100100021018_eng.pdf>.

Incorporate land acknowledgment once students have learned on whose territory the school and place-based learning location are located. The following example can be used for guidance:

- We would like to acknowledge that we are gathered today on the traditional, ancestral, and unceded territory of the _____ people.

When incorporating Indigenous perspectives, it is important to value Traditional Ecological Knowledge (TEK):

> Traditional Ecological Knowledge, or TEK, is the most popular term to denote the vast local knowledge First Peoples have about the natural world found in their traditional environment.... TEK is, above all, local knowledge based in people's relationship to place. It is also holistic, not subject to the segmentation of contemporary science. Knowledge about a specific plant may include understanding its life cycle, its spiritual connections, its relationship to the seasons and with other plants and animals in its ecosystem, as well as its uses and its stories. (*Science First Peoples Teacher Resource Guide*)

Indigenous peoples developed technologies and survived on this land for millennia because of their knowledge of the land. Indigenous peoples used observation and experimentation to refine technologies, such as building canoes and longhouses and discovering food-preservation techniques. As such, TEK serves as an invaluable resource for students and teachers of science.

Indigenous peoples do not view their knowledges as "science" but, rather, from a more holistic perspective, as is reflected in this quote from Dr. Jolly, Cherokee, and President of the Science Museum of Minnesota:

> When I weave a basket, I talk about the different dyes and how you make them and how the Oklahoma clay that we put on our baskets doesn't permeate the cell walls, it deposits on the outside. It makes a very nice dye but if you cut through the reed you'll see white still on the inside of the reed, whereas if I make a walnut dye and if I use as my mordent, alum and I use as my acid cider, that walnut dye will permeate the cell walls. You cut through the reed and it's brown through and through. Now what I've just described is the difference between osmosis and dialysis. That Western science calls those scientific terms is really wonderful, but it's not scientific terms if you are a basket weaver. Our culture incorporates so much of what people would call scientific knowledge and ways of thinking so naturally that we haven't parsed it out and put it in a book and said this is our science knowledge versus our weaver's knowledge. When I weave a basket I also tell the stories of the spirituality and not just the ways in which I dyed it. A basket weaver is as much a scientist as an artist, and a spiritual teacher. We'd never think that you'd separate out just the science part, but you can't weave a basket without knowing the science. (*Science First Peoples Teacher Resource Guide*)

Throughout **Hands-On Science**, there are many opportunities to incorporate culturally appropriate teaching methodologies from an Indigenous worldview. First Peoples Pedagogy indicates that making connections to the local community is central to learning (*Science First Peoples Teacher Resource Guide*). As one example, Elders and Knowledge Keepers offer a wealth of knowledge that can be shared with students. Consider inviting a local Elder or Knowledge Keeper as a guest into the classroom in connection with specific topics being studied (as identified within the given lessons throughout the module). An Elder or Knowledge Keeper can guide a nature walk, share stories and experiences, share traditional technologies, and help students understand Indigenous peoples' perspectives of the natural world. Elders and Knowledge Keepers will provide guidance for learners and opportunities to build bridges between the school and the community.

Here are a few suggestions about working with Elders and Knowledge Keepers:

- Elders and Knowledge Keepers have a deep spirituality that influences every aspect of their lives and teachings. They are recognized because they have earned the respect of their community through wisdom, harmony, and balance in their actions and teachings. (See: "Aboriginal Elder Definition" at <https://www.ictinc.ca/blog/aboriginal-elder-definition>).
- Some Indigenous keepers of knowledge are more comfortable being called "Knowledge Keepers" than "Elders." Be sensitive to their preference. In many communities, there are also "Junior Elders" who may also be invited to share their knowledge with students and school staff.
- Elders and Knowledge Keepers may wish to speak about what seems appropriate to them, instead of being directed to talk about something specific. It is important to respect this choice and not be directive about what an Elder or Knowledge Keeper will talk about during their visit.
- It is important to properly acknowledge any visiting Elders or Knowledge Keepers and their knowledge, as they have traditionally

been and are recognized within Indigenous communities as highly esteemed individuals. There are certain protocols that should be followed when inviting an Elder or Knowledge Keeper to support student learning in the classroom or on the land. The *Science First Peoples Teacher Resource Guide* offers guidelines and considerations for this.

It is especially important to connect with Indigenous communities, Elders, and Knowledge Keepers in your local area, and to study local issues related to Indigenous peoples in British Columbia. Consider contacting Indigenous education consultants within your local school district or with the British Columbia Ministry of Education to access referrals. The following link provides a province-wide list of Indigenous contacts: <www.bced.gov.bc.ca/apps/imcl/imclWeb/AB.do>. Also, consider contacting local Indigenous organizations for referrals to Elders and Knowledge Keepers. Such organizations may also be able to offer resources and opportunities for field trips and place-based learning.

NOTE: It is important for educators to understand the significant contribution that Elders, Knowledge Keepers, and Indigenous communities make when they share their traditional knowledge. In their culture of reciprocity, this understanding should extend past giving a gift or honorarium to an Elder or Knowledge Keeper for sharing sacred knowledge. As such, educators should think deeply about reciprocity and what they can do beyond inviting Indigenous guests to their classrooms. Educators can expand their own learning and become connected to Indigenous people by, for example, engaging in Indigenous community events, working with the Education Department of the local Nations, or exploring ways to continue developing the relationship between the local Nations and educators in the district.

The First Nations Education Steering Committee of British Columbia has articulated the following **First Peoples Principles of Learning**:

- Learning ultimately supports the well-being of the self, the family, the community, the land, the spirits, and the ancestors.
- Learning is holistic, reflexive, reflective, experiential, and relational (focused on connectedness, on reciprocal relationships, and a sense of place).
- Learning involves recognizing the consequences of one's actions.
- Learning involves generational roles and responsibilities.
- Learning recognizes the role of Indigenous knowledge.
- Learning is embedded in memory, history, and story.
- Learning involves patience and time.
- Learning requires exploration of one's identity.
- Learning involves recognizing that some knowledge is sacred and only shared with permission and/or in certain situations.

These principles generally reflect First Peoples pedagogy, and have been considered in the development of **Hands-On Science**:

> The First People Principles of Learning (FPPL) is a framework for approaching learning, or a worldview on what learning is and how it happens. Teachers are encouraged to find their own meaning in them, explore them with their class, and take them up in a way that is meaningful to them. They are embedded in the new curriculum—the new curriculum was created based on these principles. Teachers can make their own connections to the FPPL through the **Hands-On Science** resource. (Melanie Nelson, February 12, 2018)

It is also important to note that the *Science First Peoples Teacher Resource Guide* recommends a 7E model for guiding experiential learning activities in science. This model suggests that the following elements are essential to the learning experience:

The 7E Model

Environment	▪ using the local land (place-based learning)
Engage	▪ inspiring curiosity and activating knowledge
Explore	▪ investigating science concepts through hands-on experiences
Elders	▪ connecting local Knowledge Keepers to learning
Explain	▪ describing observations and sharing new knowledge
Elaborate	▪ extending and enhancing learning
Evaluation	▪ providing opportunities for students to demonstrate understanding and skills

These seven elements are strongly evident in the approach used in **Hands-On Science**, as is explained in the following sections.

For more information on First Peoples Pedagogy and First Peoples Principles of Learning, please see the *Science First Peoples Teacher Resource Guide*.

NOTE: Indigenous resources recommended in **Hands-On Science** are considered to be authentic resources, meaning that they reference the Indigenous community they came from, they state the individual who shared the story and gave permission for the story to be used publicly, and the person who originally shared the story is Indigenous. Stories that are works of fiction were written by an Indigenous author. For more information, please see *Authentic First Peoples Resources* at: <www.fnesc.ca/learningfirstpeoples/>.

References

"Aboriginal Contacts—Basic Information." British Columbia Ministry of Education. Accessed 30 October 2018. <www.bced.gov.bc.ca/apps/imcl/imclWeb/AB.do>

Banchi, Heather, and Randi Bell. "The Many Levels of Inquiry." *Science and Children*, 46.2 (2008): 26–29.

British Columbia Ministry of Education. *BC's New Curriculum.* 2016. <https://curriculum.gov.bc.ca/>

"First Nations in British Columbia." Indigenous Services Canada. <https://www.aadnc-aandc.gc.ca/DAM/DAM-INTER-BC/STAGING/texte-text/fnmp_1100100021018_eng.pdf>

"Aboriginal Elder Definition." Indigenous Corporate Training, Inc., 2012. <https://www.ictinc.ca/blog/aboriginal-elder-definition>

"Learning First Peoples Classroom Resources." First Nations Education Steering Committee. <http://www.fnesc.ca/learningfirstpeoples/> (includes the *First Peoples Principles of Learning* and *Authentic First Peoples Resources*)

Mack, E., H. Augare, L. Different Cloud-Jones, D. David, H. Quiver Gaddie, R. Honey, & R. Wippert. "Effective practices for creating transformative informal science education programs grounded in Native ways of knowing." *Cultural Studies of Science Education*, 7, 49-70. 2012.

Truth and Reconciliation Commission of Canada: Calls to Action. Truth and Reconciliation Commission of Canada, 2015. <http://www.trc.ca/websites/trcinstitution/File/2015/Findings/Calls_to_Action_English2.pdf>

Science First Peoples Teacher Resource Guide. First Nations Education Steering Committee and First Nations Schools Association, 2016.

How to Use *Hands-On Science* in Your Classroom

Hands-On Science is organized in a format that makes it easy for teachers to plan and implement. Four modules address the selected topics of study for kindergarten to grade-two classrooms. The modules relate directly to the Big Ideas, Core Competencies, Curricular Competencies, and Content outlined in the Science Curriculum for British Columbia.

Multi-Age Teaching and Learning

Whether working with students in a single-grade classroom from kindergarten to grade two, or working with multi-age classes, teachers will find appropriate learning opportunities in *Hands-On Science*. The lessons meet the diverse needs of all students through the implementation of differentiated instruction and personalized learning.

The Science Curriculum for British Columbia establishes specific Big Ideas, Curricular Competencies, and Content for each grade level. *Hands-On Science* has worked within themes to infuse these Big Ideas, Curricular Competencies, and Content into multi-age modules (see the Curriculum Learning Framework at the beginning of each module). It is therefore important for teachers to work collaboratively with their colleagues across grade levels to determine how best to implement lessons. The Curriculum Learning Frameworks will also be helpful, as each one includes a grade-level focus for specific lessons. This will assist teachers in both single-grade classrooms or multi-age classrooms to identify lessons and topics appropriate to their class.

Differentiated instruction and personalized learning will also ensure the needs of all students are met during science lessons. For example, in any classroom, whether multi-age or single-grade, students will be working at varying levels of literacy. As such, some students may be communicating their learning through drawing, while others may use single words, and yet others write several sentences. The lessons in *Hands-On Science* are developed to foster growth and learning at all literacy levels.

The same situation may be evident in terms of numeracy. For example, some students may be using comparative nonstandard measurement, while other students may be capable of working with standard metric measurement units and devices. There is plenty of flexibility in *Hands-On Science* to ensure that all students' learning needs can be met through active, student-centred learning.

Module Overview

Each module features an overarching question that fosters inquiry related to the Big Ideas. The module also has its own introduction, which summarizes the general concepts and goals for the module. This introduction provides background information for teachers, planning tips, and lists of vocabulary related to the module, as well as other pertinent information (e.g., how to embed Indigenous perspectives).

Also included at the beginning of each module is a Curriculum Learning Framework, which is based on the Big Ideas and Learning Standards (Curricular Competencies and Content) from the Science Curriculum for British Columbia (https://curriculum.gov.bc.ca/).

The Curriculum Learning Framework identifies the Big Ideas, Sample Guided Inquiry Questions, and Content for each grade level. As well, Content is connected to specific lessons, which are listed below each Content concept. Although specific lessons were intentionally written for grade-level content, much of this content is interconnected. As such, the overarching theme of the module provides a variety of connections to all three grade levels and, therefore, offers many springboards to learning.

Lesson Title
- provides a guided inquiry question related to the Learning Standards explored in the lesson

Information for Teachers
- presents basic scientific knowledge needed for activities

Explore
- presents whole-class and small-group activities which provide students with choice and opportunities to pose further inquiry questions while collaborating with peers
- details procedures, including higher-level questioning techniques, and suggestions for encouraging the development of concepts and skills
- identified as Explore Part One, Explore Part Two, and so on (when there is more than one in a lesson)

Expand
- provides opportunities for individual students to expand what they know, do, and understand
- empowers and encourages students to pose their own inquiry questions and conduct investigations, research, and projects individually, with support and facilitation by the teacher as needed; student success will depend on prior modelling, guided practice, and individual skills
- includes suggestions for Makerspace projects and Loose Parts exploration

Learning Centre
- supports diverse learners, promotes differentiated instruction, and is based on multiple-intelligences research (see page 17)
- includes a task card that remains at the centre, along with any required supplies and materials; review the task card before students work at the centre, to ensure they are familiar with the content and the expectations (students are not expected to read and comprehend all content on the card, but it serves as a guide for teachers and a visual prompt for students)

---

1 Initiating Event: What Do We Observe, Think, and Wonder About Plants and Animals?

Information for Teachers

In this lesson, students will participate in place-based learning to explore plants and animals in a local natural environment. Encourage students to suggest local natural areas, and plan ahead to select a location.

NOTE: It is important to prepare for guest speakers and to ensure that students are appropriately prepared as well. Review behavioural expectations and discuss questions that students may wish to ask the guest. Be sure to have students thank the speaker for the visit and consider following up with written or illustrated thank you notes. It is also important to consider protocols for Elders. Please see the *Science First Peoples Teacher Resource Guide* (see References, page xx) for guidelines and considerations.

In preparing to explore nature with students, consider referring to the book, *A Place for Wonder: Reading and Writing Nonfiction in the Primary Grades*, by Georgia Heard and Jennifer McDonough (see References, page xxx).

Materials
- chart paper
- markers
- digital cameras
- magnifying glasses
- tweezers
- stretch gloves
- recycled bags
- string
- portable whiteboard or chart paper with a sturdy backboard

Engage

Discuss the location for the place-based learning. Ask:
- Who has been to this place before?
- How did you get there?
- What is it like there?
- What do you think we will see there? Smell? Hear? Feel?

Introduce the guided inquiry question: **What do we observe, think, and wonder about plants and animals?**

Explore Part One

Once the class has arrived at the place-based learning location, provide time for students to explore the area freely (under adult supervision). Provide access to materials such as digital cameras, magnifying glasses, tweezers, stretch gloves, garden tools for exploration, and recycled bags in which to collect artifacts.

As students explore, pose questions for them to ponder. For example:
- What are you examining?
- Why is it interesting to you?
- What can you tell me about it?
- What do you wonder about it?
- What do you see? Feel? Smell? Hear?

Expand

To prepare students for journaling, do a journal entry together as a class. This will require a portable whiteboard and markers, or chart paper with a sturdy backboard.

- sketching or colouring plants and animals in the natural environment
- collecting flowers or leaves, sketching them, and then pressing them in the journal

Learning Centre

At the learning centre, provide a variety of objects and photographs collected during the place-based learning experience. Also provide magnifying glasses, tweezers, scissors, glue, art paper, poster paper, construction paper, art supplies, and a copy of the Learning-Centre

---

Materials
- lists all materials required to conduct the main activities
- includes items for display purposes or for recording students' ideas
- suggests visual materials (e.g., large pictures, sample charts, diagrams) to assist in presenting ideas and questions and encourage discussion
- connects to Image Bank visuals, which may be printed or projected for specific activities (see Appendix on page 175 for thumbnails and free access)

Engage
- activates prior knowledge, piques students' curiosity about related concepts, and introduces the lesson's guided inquiry question
- models for students how to pose their own inquiry questions; teachers may choose to record the guided inquiry question (e.g., on a sentence strip) for display, so students can refer to it during activities and discussions

Reproducibles
- may be used to guide activities or record data
- may also serve as a template for designing and constructing graphic organizers
- included as thumbnails in the lessons
- provided as full-sized, printable version on the Portage & Main website (see Appendix for URL and password)

Enhance
- enriches and elaborates on the Big Idea, Core Competencies, and Learning Standards with optional activities
- includes interactive activities, available through the Portage & Main Press website; check this section of each lesson for directions on accessing interactive activities
- encourages active participation and learning through Family Connections

Embed Part One
- provides students with opportunities to participate in a Talking Circle (see page 16) to demonstrate their learning through consolidation and reflection
- allows for synthesis and application of inquiry and new ideas
- reviews main ideas of the lesson, focusing on the Big Idea, Core Competencies, and Learning Standards
- reviews guided inquiry question so students can share their knowledge, provide examples, and ask further inquiry questions

Embed Part Two
- embeds learning by adding to graphic organizers; having students record, describe, and illustrate new vocabulary; and adding new vocabulary to the word wall throughout the module or even all year
- provides opportunity to reflect the cultural diversity of the classroom and the community by including new terminology in languages other than English, including Indigenous languages
- explores Core Competencies with students to foster student self-assessment of how these skills were used throughout the lesson

Assessment
- provides suggestions for authentic assessment
- includes student self-assessment, formative assessment, and summative assessment (see pages 29–34)

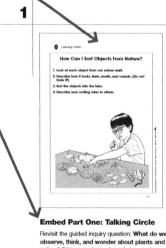

How to Use *Hands-On Science* in Your Classroom

The Curricular Competencies Correlation Chart at the beginning of each module provides details on how students' Curricular Competencies are developed through scientific inquiry. The chart outlines the skills, strategies, and processes that students use in the module and identifies the specific lessons in which these Curricular Competencies are the focus. The Curricular Competencies are developed in various ways over time, and therefore are addressed in multiple lessons throughout **Hands-On Science** modules.

Each module includes a list of related resources for students (books, websites, and online videos).

Each module is organized into lessons based on the Learning Standards. The first lesson in each module provides an initiating event, using an Observe-Think-Wonder strategy. Real-life explorations, often within the local environment, provide opportunity for place-based learning, which is discussed in more detail on page 18.

The second lesson in each module explores storytelling as it relates to the inquiry topics. This lesson includes an emphasis on Indigenous stories, children's literature, and nonfiction texts, while providing opportunities for students to engage in activities that focus on literacy and creative storytelling.

The last lesson in each module provides an opportunity for personalized learning through individualized inquiry, as students explore what more they would like to know, do, and understand about the module's Big Ideas.

Talking Circles

Talking Circles originated with First Nations leaders as a process to encourage dialogue, respect, and the co-construction of ideas. The following process is generally used in a Talking Circle:

- the group forms a complete circle
- one person holds an object such as a stick, feather, shell, or stone
- only the person holding the stick talks, while the rest listen
- the stick is passed around in a clockwise direction
- each person talks until they are finished, being respectful of time
- the Talking Circle is complete when everyone has had a chance to speak
- a person may pass the stick without speaking, if they choose

See <www.firstnationspedagogy.ca/circletalks.html> for more information. Also consider inviting a local Elder or Knowledge Keeper to share with the class the process of a Talking Circle.

Multiple Intelligences Learning Centres

Learning centres in **Hands-On Science** focus on a different multiple intelligence to provide opportunities for students to use areas of strength and also to expose them to new ways of learning.

Teachers are encouraged to explore the topic of multiple intelligences with their students and to have students self-reflect to identify ways they learn best, and ways that are challenging for them. Guidelines for this process are included in *Teaching to Diversity* by Jennifer Katz (see References, page 21).

Multiple Intelligence	These learners…
Verbal-Linguistic	…think in words and enjoy reading, writing, word puzzles, and oral storytelling.
Logical-Mathematical	…think by reasoning and enjoy problem solving, puzzles, and working with data.
Visual-Spatial	…think in visual pictures and enjoy drawing and creating visual designs.
Bodily-Kinesthetic	…think by using their physical bodies and enjoy movement, sports, dance, and hands-on activities.
Musical-Rhythmic	…think in melodies and rhythms and enjoy singing, listening to music, and creating music.
Interpersonal	…think by talking to others about their ideas and enjoy group work, planning social events, and taking a leadership role with friends or classmates.
Intrapersonal	…think within themselves and enjoy quietly thinking, reflecting, and working individually.
Naturalistic	…learn by classifying objects and events and enjoy anything to do with nature and scientific exploration of natural phenomena.
Existential	…learn by probing deep philosophical questions and enjoy examining the bigger picture as to why ideas are important.

How to Use *Hands-On Science* in Your Classroom

Icons

To provide a clear indication of important features of **Hands-On Science**, the following icons are used throughout lessons:

Place-Based Learning	Place-based learning focuses on the local environment and community. It is important for students to explore the local area in order to build personalized and contextual knowledge. Place-based learning: - emphasizes exploring the natural environment, replacing classroom walls with the natural land - offers firsthand opportunities to observe, explore, and investigate the land, waters, organisms, and atmosphere of the local region - promotes a healthy interplay between society and nature - helps students envision a world where there is meaningful appreciation and respect for our natural environment—an environment that sustains all life Many lessons in **Hands-On Science** incorporate place-based learning activities, whether it be a casual walk around the neighbourhood to examine trees or a more involved exploration of local waterways.
Applied Design, Skills, and Technologies	Throughout **Hands-On Science**, students have opportunities to use applied design, skills, and technologies to plan and construct objects. For example, in *Living Things for Grades K–2*, students design and construct models of an animal's environment to show how the animal meets its basic needs. Using applied design skills and technology, students seek solutions to practical problems through research and experimentation. There are specific steps: 1. Identify a need. Recognize practical problems and the need to solve them. 2. Create a plan. Seek alternate solutions to a given problem, create a plan based on a chosen solution, and record the plan through writing and labelled diagrams. 3. Develop a product or prototype. Construct an object that solves the given problem, and use predetermined criteria to test the product. 4. Communicate the results. Identify and make improvements to the product, and explain the changes.
Ecology and the Environment	**Hands-On Science** provides numerous opportunities for students to investigate issues related to ecology, the environment, and sustainable development. The meaning of sustainability can be clarified by asking students: "Is there enough for everyone, forever?" These topics also connect to Indigenous worldviews about respecting and caring for the Earth.
Technology	Digital learning, or information and communication technology (ICT), is an important component of any classroom. As such, technological supports available in schools—digital cameras, computers/tablets, interactive whiteboards (IWB), projectors, document cameras, audio-recording devices, calculators—can be used with and by students to enhance their learning experiences.
Classroom Safety	When there are safety concerns, teachers may decide to demonstrate an activity, while still encouraging as much student interaction as possible. The nature of science and scientific experimentation means that safety concerns do arise from time to time.

Makerspace Centres

To foster open inquiry and promote personalized learning, each module of **Hands-On Science** suggests a Makerspace centre as part of the Expand section. A Makerspace is a creative do-it-yourself environment, where participants pose questions, share ideas, and explore hands-on projects. In the school setting, a Makerspace is usually cross-curricular and should allow for inquiry, discovery, and innovation. Sometimes, the Makerspace is housed in a common area, such as the library, which means it is a space used by the whole school community. A classroom Makerspace is usually designed as a centre where students create do-it-yourself projects, emphasizing personalized learning, while collaborating with others on cross-curricular ideas. It is important to remember learning is not directed here. Rather, simply create conditions for learning to happen.

There is no list of required equipment that defines a Makerspace; however, the centre may evolve to foster inquiry within a specific topic. Students are given the opportunity to work with a variety of age-appropriate tools, as well as with everyday, arts-and-crafts, and recycled materials. Materials to consider at Makerspace centres include:

- general supplies (e.g., graph or grid paper for planning and designing, pencils, markers, paper, cardstock, cardboard, scissors, masking tape, duct tape, glue, rulers, metre sticks, tape measures, elastic bands, string, Plasticine, modelling clay, fabric/cloth, straws, pipe cleaners, aluminum foil)
- recycled materials (e.g., various sizes of boxes, cardboard rolls, milk cartons, plastic bottles, spools, plastic lids)
- art supplies (e.g., paper, paint, markers, chalk, pastels, crayons, pencil crayons, beads, sequins, foam shapes, yarn, glass beads)
- building materials (e.g., sticks, wooden blocks, wooden dowels, toothpicks, craft sticks, balsa wood)
- age-appropriate tools (e.g., hammers, nails, screwdrivers, screws)
- natural objects (e.g., rocks, shells, feathers, seeds, wood slices, sticks)
- commercial products (e.g., LEGO, LEGO Story Starter, WeDo, MakeDo, Meccano, Plus-Plus, K'Nex, KEVA Planks, Dominoes, Wedgits)
- technology (e.g., Green Screen, iPads, coding/programming [Beebots, Code-a Pillar], apps such as Hopscotch, Tynker, Scratch Jr., Tickle)
- topic-based literature to inspire projects
- reference materials (e.g., books, videos, websites, visual images)

Work with students to develop a collaborative culture in which they tinker, invent, and improve on their creations. Ask students for ideas on how to stock the Makerspace, based on their project ideas, and then work collaboratively to acquire these supplies. The internet may also provide ideas for projects and materials.

Set up a recycling box/bin in the Makerspace centre for paper, cardboard, clean plastics, and other materials students can use for their creations. Stress to students that Makerspaces can help reuse many items destined for a landfill. Discuss which items can/should be placed in this bin.

Some things to consider when planning and developing a Makerspace centre are:

- Always address safety concerns, ensuring materials, equipment, and tools are safe for student use. Include safety gloves and goggles, as appropriate. Engage students in a discussion about safety and respect at the Makerspace before beginning each module. Consider sharp objects, small parts,

and other potential hazards for students of all ages and abilities who will have access to the Makerspace centre. At this age, this exploration needs to be supervised.
- Consider space and storage needs. Mobile carts and/or bins are handy for storing raw materials and tools.
- Work with students to write a letter to parents/guardians, explaining the purpose of the Makerspace, and asking for donations of materials.

In **Hands-On Science**, each module includes a variety of suggestions for Makerspace materials, equipment, possible challenges, and literature links related to the Big Ideas being explored.

The Makerspace process is intended for solving design problems, so it is helpful to have visuals at the Makerspace centre to encourage innovation, creativity, and the use of Applied Design, Skills, and Technologies (see page 18). In addition, although individual inquiry is encouraged, the Makerspace process is often collaborative in nature. Therefore, it is important to focus on skills related to working with others (see the Cooperative Skills Assessment templates on pages 49 and 51).

Before students begin working at a Makerspace centre, review Applied Design, Skills, and Technologies and collaborative skills with students. As a class, co-construct criteria for each skill, record on chart paper, and display at the Makerspace centre. Or, challenge students to create posters for the Makerspace centre that convey what Applied Design, Skills, and Technologies and collaboration look like. Refer to these visual prompts before, during, and after students work at the centre, as a means of guiding and assessing the process.

As students create, photograph their creations to share with the class, and discuss the unique properties of their designs. Model appropriate digital citizenship with students by asking their permission to photograph and share their creations. Facilitate regular debriefing sessions as a class, after students have spent time at the Makerspace centre. Consider focusing this discussion on the Core Competencies (Thinking, Communication, and Personal and Social Skills) as an anchor for reflective practice.

The nature of a Makerspace is such that it provides an excellent venue for personalized learning. As students pose their own inquiry questions, they may choose to use the Makerspace to explore that question further.

Loose Parts

Closely related to the open inquiry fostered by the Makerspace, the theory of Loose Parts was first proposed back in the 1970s by architect Simon Nicholson. He believed it is the Loose Parts in our environment that empower our creativity. The theory has begun to influence early years educators intent on offering students opportunities to play freely with objects and materials, and to pose their own questions and investigations. Loose Parts include anything natural or synthetic (e.g., beads, buttons, fabric, washers and nuts, cardboard rolls, pom poms, acorns, leaves) that students can move, control, and manipulate. Loose Parts promote open-ended thinking that leads to problem solving, curiosity, and creativity. Play and learning possibilities are endless, as there is no single outcome that is achieved. Instead, Loose Parts offer opportunities for students to consider a wide range of possibilities and ideas.

When appropriate, provide provocations (questions to inspire play) that offer an entry point for a Loose Parts activity. As an example, while studying living things, teachers may provide bins of stones, twigs, bark, shells, and seed pods with the provocation, "How many different ways can you sort the objects?"

Students may begin with such a sorting task, but expand to build structures, compare and measure, or examine patterns on the various objects.

Throughout **Hands-On Science**, Loose Parts are used to engage students and as an opportunity to expand investigations, generate their own inquiry questions, and personalize learning. Suggestions for Loose Parts exploration are included in the Expand section of lessons. For more information about Loose Parts, see *Loose Parts: Inspiring Play in Young Children* by Lisa Daly and Miriam Beloglovsky and *Loose Parts: A Start-Up Guide* by Sally Haughey and Nicole Hill.

References

British Columbia Ministry of Education. *BC's New Curriculum.* 2016. <https://curriculum.gov.bc.ca/>

Daly, Lisa, and Miriam Beloglovsky. *Loose Parts: Inspiring Play in Young Children.* Redleaf Press, 2014.

Haughey, Sally, and Nicole Hill. *Loose Parts: A Start-Up Guide.* Fairy Dust Teaching, 2017.

Katz, Jennifer. *Teaching to Diversity.* Winnipeg, MB: Portage & Main Press, 2012.

"Talking Circles." *First Nations Pedagogy Online.* <www.firstnationspedagogy.ca/circletalks.html>

Curricular Competencies: How to Infuse Scientific Inquiry Skills and Processes Into Lessons

Hands-On Science is based on a scientific inquiry approach. While participating in the activities of *Hands-On Science*, students use a variety of scientific inquiry skills and processes as they answer questions, solve problems, and make decisions. These skills and processes are not unique to science, but they are integral to students' acquisition of scientific literacy. At the kindergarten to grade-two level, these include:

QP	questioning and predicting
PC	planning and conducting
PA	processing and analyzing data and information
AI	applying and innovating
C	communicating
E	evaluating

The icons above are used to link assessment suggestions to Curricular Competencies (see page 33 for more information).

Use the following guidelines to encourage the development of students' skills and processes in specific areas.

Observing

Students learn to perceive characteristics and changes through the use of all five senses. Encourage students to safely use sight, smell, touch, hearing, and taste to gain information about objects and events. Observations may be qualitative (e.g., texture, colour), quantitative (e.g., size, number), or both.

Observing includes:

- gaining information through the senses
- identifying similarities and differences, and making comparisons

Encourage students to communicate their observations in a variety of ways, including orally, in writing, by sketching labelled diagrams, and by capturing evidence digitally (e.g., with a digital camera).

Questioning

Generating thoughtful inquiry questions is an essential skill for students when participating in inquiry-based learning. Encourage students to be curious and to extend their questions beyond those posed to them.

Students should learn to formulate a specific question to investigate, one that can be answered through experimentation. This skill takes time to develop with young learners. Be patient, and provide the appropriate scaffolds as needed. Then students can create, from a variety of possible methods, a plan to find answers to the questions they pose.

Exploring

Students need ample opportunity to manipulate materials and equipment in order to discover and learn new ideas and concepts. During exploration, encourage students to use all of their senses and observation skills.

Oral discussion is an integral component of exploration; it allows students to communicate their discoveries. At a deeper level, discussion also allows students to make meaning by discussing inconsistencies and by comparing/contrasting their observations with others. This is the constructivist model of learning, which is essential in inquiry-based learning. It is also essential to document the learning that is taking place for each child. This can be done through anecdotal observation records, photographs, videos, and interviews.

Classifying

Classification is used to group or sort objects and events, and is based on observable properties. For example, objects can be classified into groups according to colour, shape, or size. Two strategies for sorting include sorting mats and Venn diagrams. Sorting mats show distinct groups, while Venn diagrams intersect to show similar characteristics among sets.

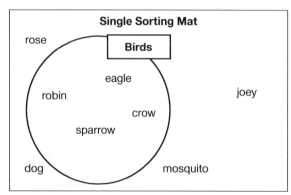

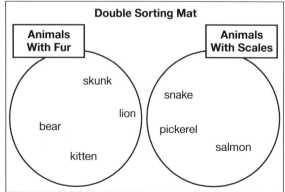

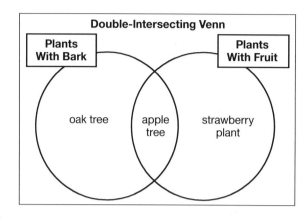

Measuring

Measuring is the process of discovering the dimensions or the quantity of objects or events and, at the kindergarten to grade-one level, usually involves comparing and ordering objects by length, area, volume, and mass. Measuring activities first involve the use of nonstandard units of measure (e.g., interlocking cubes, paper clips) to determine length. At the kindergarten to grade-one level, students generally use only nonstandard units to make simple measurements, as they build understanding of how to observe, compare, and communicate dimensions and quantity. This is a critical preface to measuring with standard units. By grade two, and/or in cases where students have demonstrated competence with nonstandard measurement, students may be introduced to standard units (e.g., centimetres, metres, grams, kilograms) and the use of measuring devices (e.g., metre sticks, tape measures, spring scales, calibrated beakers).

An essential skill of measurement is estimating. Encourage students to estimate before they measure, whether in nonstandard or standard units. Estimation gives students opportunities to take risks, use background knowledge, and enhance their measuring skills by comparing estimates and actual results.

Communicating, Analyzing, and Interpreting

In science, communication is achieved through diagrams, graphs, charts, maps, models, and symbols, as well as with written and spoken languages. At the kindergarten to grade-two level, communicating includes:

- viewing images
- making labelled diagrams*
- journaling
- reading and interpreting data from simple tables and charts
- making tables and charts
- reading and interpreting data from pictographs
- making pictographs
- making models
- using oral languages
- sequencing and grouping events, objects, and data according to attributes

*** NOTE:** Depending on students' literacy skills, they may label diagrams with letters and words. Model this to show that a scientific diagram includes accurate illustrations, labels, and sometimes measurements.

Journaling is an important strategy that offers students an opportunity to communicate their ideas, understandings, and questions through emergent writing and illustrating. A journal can be used to summarize activities, share new knowledge, or record observations.

A journal is especially useful during place-based learning experiences. Scientists, such as Charles Darwin, a naturalist, and Rachel Carson, a marine biologist and conservationist, used this strategy for recording observations. The **place-based journal** encourages students to slow down, pay attention to the world around them, heighten their senses, observe more accurately, and reflect on experiences (Bell, 2017). See About This Module, page 60, for more information.

Other forms of communication in science include reading and interpreting charts and graphs. When presenting students with charts and graphs, or when students make their own as part of a specific activity, there are guidelines that should be followed:

- A **pictograph** has a title and information on one axis that denotes the items being compared (note that the first letter of each word on both the title and the axis text is capitalized). There is generally no graduated scale or heading for the axis representing numerical values.

Favourite Dessert				
		🍦		
		🍦		
	🥧	🍦		
🎂	🥧	🍦		
Cake	Pie	Ice Cream		

- A **tally chart** is a means of recording data as an organized count. The count is grouped in fives for ease of determining the total by counting by fives.

Favourite Sport		
Sport	Tally	Total
baseball	ⵘ I	6
hockey	ⵘ ⵘ	10
soccer	ⵘ ⵘ II	12

- A **chart (table)** requires an appropriate title, and both columns and rows need specific headings. Again, all titles and headings require capitalization of the first letter of each word, as in the title of a story. In some cases, pictures can be used to make the chart easier for young students to understand. Charts can be made in the form of checklists or can include room for additional written information and data.

Checklist Chart

Which Substances Dissolve in Water?		
Substance	Dissolves in Water	Does Not Dissolve in Water
Beads		√
Sugar	√	
Drink Mix	√	
Rice		√
Pepper		√

Data Chart

Local Snowfall		
Month	2016/2017 Snowfall (cm)	Average Snowfall (cm)
October	7	5
November	9	8
December	23	20
January	29	25
February	16	18
March	11	10

Communicating also involves using the language and terminology of science. Encourage students to use the appropriate vocabulary related to their investigations (e.g., *object, metal, heavy, strong, movement*). The language of science also includes terms such as *predict, infer, estimate, measure, experiment*, and *hypothesize*. Use this vocabulary regularly throughout all activities and encourage students to do the same. In each module, work with students to develop a word wall on which to record terms students have learned. Have students provide visuals, and define the terms in their own words.

Predicting

Predicting refers to the question, "What do you think will happen?" For example, ask students to predict what they think will happen to an inflated balloon that is placed in a basin of water. It is important to provide opportunities for students to make predictions and to feel safe doing so.

Inferring

In a scientific context, inferring refers to deducing why something occurs. For example, ask students to infer why an inflated balloon floats when placed into a basin of water. Again, it is important to encourage students to take risks when making inferences. Instead of explaining scientific phenomena to them, give students opportunities to infer for themselves, using a variety of perspectives, and then build their knowledge base through inquiry and investigation.

Inquiry Through Investigation and Experimentation

When investigations and experiments are conducted in the classroom, planning and recording both the process and the results are essential. The traditional scientific method uses the following format:

- **purpose:** what we want to find out, or a testable question we want to answer
- **hypothesis:** a prediction; what we think will happen, and why
- **materials:** what we used to conduct the experiment or investigation
- **method:** what we did
- **results:** what we observed and measured
- **conclusion:** what we found out
- **application:** how we can use what we learned

This method of recording investigations may be used in later school years. However, in the early grades, it may be more appropriate to focus on a narrative style of reporting such as:

- what we want to know
- what we think might happen
- what we used
- what we did
- what we observed
- what we found out

A simpler four-question narrative may also be used with any age group. The structure includes the following questions:

- What was I looking for? (Describe the question you were trying to answer, or the hypothesis/prediction you were testing.)
- How did I look for it? (Tell what you did. Include materials and method.)
- What did I find? (Describe observations and data.)
- What does this mean? (Draw conclusions, and consider applications to real life.)

This narrative may be done in a variety of ways: oral discussion as a class, recording findings as a class, having students use drawings, or a combination of these.

Throughout **Hands-On Science**, a variety of methods are used to encourage students to communicate the inquiry process, including those above. Other formats such as concept maps and other graphic organizers are also used.

Inquiry Through Research

In addition to hands-on inquiry, research is another aspect of inquiry that involves finding, organizing, and presenting information related to a specific topic or question. Scientific inquiry involves making observations, exploring, asking questions, and looking for answers to those questions. Even at a young age, students can begin to research topics studied in class if they are provided with support and guidelines.

Accordingly, guided research is a teaching and learning strategy encouraged throughout **Hands-On Science**. Guided research provides an opportunity for students to seek further information about subjects of inquiry, personal interests, or topics of their choice. As such, students are empowered and engaged in the process.

Guided research encourages students and teachers to do the following:

Students	Teachers
ask questions of interest related to a topic being studied by the class	provide opportunities for students to ask questions of personal interest
choose resources	provide access to resources
collect information	
make a plan to present findings	model and support the research process
present research in a variety of ways	offer opportunities for students to present their findings in a variety of ways and to a variety of audiences

In **Hands-On Science**, the approach to inquiry and research is one of gradual release. In order to provide more opportunity for success and independence in conducting research, it is important to scaffold the process. Consider using gradual release of responsibility (Regie Routman, 2008) as a learning model for research:

I Do It	■ Begin by modeling the process. Select an inquiry question and demonstrate how to choose resources. ■ Use the resources available in the class science library. Also use selected websites appropriate for your students (see Resources for Students at the beginning of each module). ■ Next, demonstrate how to collect information through note taking (jot notes), labelled diagrams, pictures, or photographs. ■ Finally, make a plan to present and display findings for the class.
We Do It	■ Next, have the class choose another inquiry question. ■ Together, choose resources and collect information. ■ Together, make a plan to present findings and display findings for another class or for family/community members.
You Do It	■ Students now choose their own inquiry questions, conduct research, and present findings.

Throughout this gradual release process, the teacher provides substantial support in initial inquiry experiences and, over time, presents students with more and more opportunities for directing their own research.

NOTE: Given that this module of *Hands-On Science* was developed for students in kindergarten to grade two, research needs to be age-appropriate. Collect a variety of resources at early reading levels, including visuals, books, and websites. Students can then access information and record their ideas using pictures, labelled diagrams, and simple texts, such as jot notes. If, for example, a student is researching how an eagle builds a nest, they may examine a variety of pictures, books, websites, and videos, and then create a series of labelled drawings to present their findings.

As students build research skills and progress through the grades, research will increase in sophistication. The guided approach and the I Do, We Do, You Do model will support students with independent inquiry as they continue to do scientific research in higher grades. For more information about this model (also known as the Optimal Learning Model), see *Teaching Essentials: Expecting the Most and Getting the Best from Every Learner, K-8* by Regie Routman, "Gradual Release of Responsibility: I do, We do, You do" by E. Levy, and "Teaching New Concepts: 'I Do It, We Do It, You Do It' Method" by A. McCoy.

Addressing Students' Early Literacy Needs

The inquiry process involves having students ask questions and conduct investigations and research to answer these questions. At the kindergarten to grade-two level, students will benefit from literacy support while conducting research. Consider having volunteers, student mentors, or educational assistants provide support during these processes to help young students conduct appropriate research and communicate their findings orally or visually. Also consider conducting brief lessons on how to read and glean information from pictures when investigating questions through the inquiry process. As well, students can show their learning through labelled pictures, invented/temporary spelling, or the use of technology that allows them to record their research orally.

Online Considerations

As our technological world continues to expand at an accelerating rate, and information is increasingly available online, students will turn to the internet more and more to expand their learning. Accordingly, **Hands-On Science** is replete with opportunities for students to use online resources for research and investigation. Discuss online safety protocols with students. Be vigilant in supervising student use of the internet. Similarly, review websites and bookmark those appropriate for student use. ▶

Also discuss plagiarism with students: copying information word for word—whether from a book, the internet, or another resource—is wrong. Such information should always be paraphrased in the student's own words, and the source of the information cited. Photographs, drawings, figures, and other images found online should also only be used with permission and citation of the source. Alternatively, students can source images for which permission has already been granted, such as through Creative Commons. Creative Commons is a non-profit organization that "promotes and enables the sharing of knowledge and creativity…[and which] produces and maintains a free suite of licensing tools to allow anyone to easily share, reuse, and remix materials with a fair 'some rights reserved' approach to copyright." See <creativecommons.org>.

References

Banchi, Heather, and Randi Bell. "The Many Levels of Inquiry," *Science and Children* 46.2 (2008): 26–29.

Bell, Antonella. *Nature Journaling*. University of Alberta, 2017.

British Columbia Ministry of Education. *BC's New Curriculum.* 2016. <https://curriculum.gov.bc.ca/>

Creative Commons. <creativecommons.org>

Davies, Anne. *Making Classroom Assessment Work* (3rd ed.). Courtenay, BC: Connections Publishing, 2011.

First Nations Schools Association. *Science First Peoples Teacher Resource Guide* (2016).

Fullan, Michael. *Great to Excellent: Launching the Next Stage of Ontario's Education Agenda* (2013).

Levy, E. (2007). Gradual Release of Responsibility: I do, We do, You do. <www.sjboces.org/doc/Gifted/GradualReleaseResponsibilityJan08.pdf>

Katz, Jennifer. *Teaching to Diversity: The Three-Block Model of Universal Design for Learning*. Winnipeg: Portage & Main Press, 2012.

Manitoba Education and Training. *Kindergarten to Grade 4 Science: Manitoba Curriculum Framework of Outcomes*, 1999. (See: <www.edu.gov.mb.ca/>)

McCoy, Antoine (2011, March 4). Teaching New Concepts: "I Do It, We Do It, You Do It" Method. <antoinemccoy.com/teaching-new-concepts>

Ontario Literacy and Numeracy Secretariat. "Inquiry-based Learning," Capacity Building series 32, p. 4 (May 2013).

Routman, Regie. *Teaching Essentials: Expecting the Most and Getting the Best from Every Learner, K–8*. Portsmouth, NH: Heinemann, 2008.

Toulouse, Pamela. *Achieving Aboriginal Student Success*. Winnipeg: Portage & Main Press, 2011.

Truth and Reconciliation Commission of Canada: *Calls to Action*, 2015. <www.trc.ca>

The *Hands-On Science* Assessment Plan

Hands-On Science provides a variety of assessment tools that enable teachers to build a comprehensive and authentic daily assessment plan for students. Based on current research about the value of quality classroom assessment (Davies, 2011), suggestions are provided for authentic assessment, which includes student self-assessment and reporting of Core Competencies.

British Columbia's K–12 Assessment System (see <https://curriculum.gov.bc.ca/assessment-system> and <https://curriculum.gov.bc.ca/classroom-assessment-and-reporting>) states:

> Assessment and curriculum are interconnected. Curriculum sets the learning standards that give focus to classroom instruction and assessment. Assessment involves the wide variety of methods or tools that educators use to identify student learning needs, measure competency acquisition, and evaluate students' progress toward meeting provincial learning standards.
>
> [British Columbia's] assessment system is being redesigned to align with the new curriculum. Assessment of all forms will support a more flexible, personalized approach to learning and measure deeper, complex thinking. [British Columbia's] educational assessment system strives to support student learning by providing timely, meaningful information on student learning through multiple forms of assessment. The assessment system has three programs:
>
> 1. Classroom Assessment and Reporting
> 2. Provincial Assessment
> 3. National and International Assessment
>
> Classroom assessment is an integral part of the instructional process and can serve as a meaningful source of information about student learning. Feedback from ongoing assessment in the classroom can be immediate and personal for a learner and guide the learner to understand their [strengths and challenges] and use the information to set new learning goals.

The primary purpose of assessment is to improve student learning. *Hands-On Science* provides assessment suggestions, rubrics, and templates for use during the teaching/learning process. These assessment suggestions include tasks related to *student self-assessment* of the Core Competencies, as well as *formative assessment* and *summative assessment* by the teacher.

Student self-assessment helps students develop their capacity to set their own goals, monitor their own progress, determine their next steps in learning, and reflect on their learning in relation to the three Core Competencies—Thinking, Communication, and Social and Personal.

Formative assessment requires that teachers provide students with descriptive feedback and coaching for improvement in relation to the Learning Standards (Curricular Competencies and Content).

Summative Assessment is comprehensive in nature, and is intended to identify student progress in relation to the Learning Standards (Curricular Competencies and Content).

Both summative and formative assessments are an integral part of a balanced classroom assessment plan. Then, when student self-assessment is infused in this assessment plan, a clearer picture emerges of where a student is in relation to the Core Competencies and Learning Standards.

Student Self-Assessment

It is important for students to reflect on their own learning. For this purpose, a variety of assessment templates are provided in *Hands-On Science*. Depending on their literacy levels, students may complete self-assessments in various ways. For example, the templates may be used as guides for oral conferences between teacher and student, or an adult may act as a scribe for the student, recording their responses.

As well, students can show their learning through labelled pictures, invented/temporary spelling, and writing, with guidance and support as needed.

For the purpose of self-assessment, find a STUDENT SELF-ASSESSMENT template, on page 35, as well as a STUDENT REFLECTIONS template on page 36.

The SCIENCE JOURNAL, on page 37, will encourage students to reflect on their own learning. Print several copies for each student, cut the pages in half, add a cover, and bind the pages together. Students can then create their own title pages for their journals. For variety, have students use the blank reverse side of each page for other reflections, such as drawing or writing about:

- new challenges
- favourite activities
- real-life experiences
- new terminology
- new places explored during investigations

Students may also journal in other ways, such as by adding notes to their portfolios, or by keeping online science blogs or journals to record successes, challenges, and next steps related to learning goals.

NOTE: This SCIENCE JOURNAL template is provided as a suggestion, but journals can also be made from simple notebooks or recycled paper.

Another component of student self-assessment involves opportunities for students to reflect on their use of the Core Competencies. During each lesson, spend time discussing and reflecting on one of the Core Competencies. The intent here is to enhance students' ability to recognize how and when they use the competencies during the inquiry process. Reflection on Core Competencies is ongoing, since students' strengths and challenges in using the Core Competencies may differ across contexts and activities.

For the purpose of this assessment process, project a copy of one of the five CORE COMPETENCY DISCUSSION PROMPTS templates on page 38–42 (one each on Communication, Creative Thinking, Critical Thinking, Positive Personal and Cultural Identity, and Personal Awareness and Responsibility). Choose one or two "I Can" statements on which to focus discussion. Students then use the "I Can" statements to provide evidence of how they demonstrated that competency (model this process for the class). For example, a student might say:

- I can ask and answer questions. I know this because I asked lots of questions about the Sun. I also answered questions about how to stay safe by wearing sunscreen, sunglasses, and hats.

The intent is to provide an opportunity for group discussion and modelling, while encouraging individual students to reflect on their use of the Core Competencies. Choose the Core Competencies and facets that are most appropriate for each lesson. There is lots of room for differentiating based on the strengths and needs of the class.

NOTE: Although the facets are identified on these templates, they are featured only for teacher reference. Students are not expected to refer to the facets during reflective discussion.

To inspire students to further reflect on each Core Competency, use a variety of self-reflection prompts. For this purpose, use the CORE COMPETENCY SELF-REFLECTION FRAMES on pages 43–47 throughout the learning process. There are five frames provided to address the Core Competencies, one each on Communication, Creative Thinking, Critical Thinking, Positive Personal and Cultural Identity, and Personal Awareness and Responsibility. Conference individually with students to support self-reflection, or students may complete prompts using words and pictures.

▶

NOTE: Use the same prompts from these templates over time, to see how thinking changes across different activities.

Another component of student self-assessment utilizes the CORE COMPETENCY STUDENT REFLECTIONS: MODULE SUMMARY template, on page 48. This is completed by students at the end of a module, in order to encourage them to reflect on how their Core Competencies have developed over time. Students' reflections are recorded in the rectangle on the template. Then, the student considers next steps in learning as related to that particular Core Competency. These reflections are recorded on the arrow on the template, again, using words and drawings.

NOTE: It is important to keep in mind that the Core Competencies will only be self-assessed by students, and not directly assessed by teachers. However, teachers may conference with students in order to encourage them to think about and discuss their learning over time.

Students should also be encouraged to reflect on their cooperative group work skills, since these are directly related to Core Competencies, as well as the skills scientists use as they collaborate in team settings. For this purpose, a COOPERATIVE SKILLS SELF-ASSESSMENT template is on page 49.

Student reflections can also be done in many other ways. For example, students can:

- interview one another
- write an outline or script and make a video
- create a slide show with an audio recording

Formative Assessment

It is important to assess students' understanding before, during, and after a lesson. The information gathered helps determine students' needs in order to plan the next steps in instruction. Students may come into class with misconceptions about science concepts. By identifying what they already know, teachers can help students make connections and address any challenges.

Formative assessment provides opportunities for teachers to document evidence of each student's learning. Along with utilizing evidence gathered from photographs, videos, and digital portfolios, document evidence of learning by using the formative assessment templates provided in **Hands-On Science**.

To assess students as they work, use the formative assessment suggestions provided with many of the activities. While observing and conversing with students, use the ANECDOTAL RECORD template and/or the INDIVIDUAL STUDENT OBSERVATIONS template to record assessment data.

- **Anecdotal Record**: To gain an authentic view of a student's progress, it is critical to record observations during lessons. The ANECDOTAL RECORD template, on page 50, provides a format for recording individual or group observations.
- **Individual Student Observations**: To focus on individual students for a longer period of time, consider using the INDIVIDUAL STUDENT OBSERVATIONS template, on page 51. This template provides more space for comments and is especially useful during conferences, interviews, or individual student performance tasks. It is important to note that not every student has to be observed during the same lesson. Observations can take place over time in order to focus on each student's learning.

Formative assessment also involves the consideration of students' collaborative skills. Always assess a student's individual performance, not the work of a group. Assess how an individual student works within a group. Such skill development includes the ability to use words and actions to encourage other students,

The *Hands-On Science* Assessment Plan

contribute to group work, and use strengths and skills to complete a given task (British Columbia Ministry of Education, 2016). For this purpose, use the COOPERATIVE SKILLS TEACHER ASSESSMENT template on page 52. Use this template as a checklist or for anecdotal comments.

Both formative assessment and summative assessment include *performance assessment*. Performance assessment is planned, systematic observation and assessment based on students actually doing a specific science activity. A SAMPLE RUBRIC and a RUBRIC template for teacher use are on pages 54 and 53. For any specific activity, before the work begins, discuss and co-construct with students success criteria for completing the task. This will ensure the success criteria relate to the lesson's learning goals. Record these criteria on the rubric. Use the rubric criteria to assess student performance, using the proficiency scale from the British Columbia Ministry of Education Framework for Classroom Assessment (see References, page 34):

Emerging	The student demonstrates an initial understanding of the concepts and competencies relevant to the expected learning.
Developing	The student demonstrates a partial understanding of the concepts and competencies relevant to the expected learning.
Proficient	The student demonstrates a complete understanding of the concepts and competencies relevant to the expected learning.
Extending	The student demonstrates a sophisticated understanding of the concepts and competencies relevant to the expected learning.

Observe student during the performance task being assessed to determine their level of proficiency on each criterion (see SAMPLE RUBRIC, page 54). Share this data with students to provide descriptive feedback, and to encourage student reflection related to performance task criteria and the level of proficiency.

Summative Assessment

Summative assessment provides a summary of student progress related to the Learning Standards at a particular point in time. It is important to gather a variety of assessment data to draw conclusions about what a student knows, can do, and understands. As such, consider collecting student products, observing processes, and having conversations with students. Only the most recent and consistent evidence should be used.

Summative assessment suggestions are provided with the culminating lesson of each module of **Hands-On Science**. Use the ANECDOTAL RECORD template, found on page 50, the INDIVIDUAL STUDENT OBSERVATIONS template, found on page 51, and the RUBRIC, found on page 53, to record student results.

A student portfolio is another format that can be used for summative assessment. A portfolio is a collection of work that shows evidence of a student's learning. There are many types of portfolios—the showcase portfolio and the progress portfolio are two popular formats. *Showcase portfolios* highlight the best of students' work, with students involved in the selection of pieces and justification for choices. *Progress portfolios* reflect students' progress as their work improves and aim to demonstrate in-depth understanding of the materials over time. Select, with student input, work to include in a science portfolio or in a science section of a multi-subject portfolio. Selections should include representative samples of student work in all types of science activities.

Templates are included to organize the portfolio (PORTFOLIO TABLE OF CONTENTS, page 55, and PORTFOLIO ENTRY RECORD, page 56).

Indigenous Perspectives on Assessment

From an Indigenous perspective, assessment is community-based, qualitative, and holistic, and includes input from all the people who influence an individual student's learning—parents, caregivers, Elders, Knowledge Keepers, community members, and educators. An assessment that includes all these perspectives provides a balanced understanding of what represents success for Indigenous students and their families/community. A strong partnership between parents/guardians/communities and school improves student achievement. Be aware that some Indigenous students may feel apprehensive about a formal process of assessment; others may find that Western achievement goals do not fit their worldview.

In *Hands-On Science*, consideration has been given to assessment from an Indigenous perspective. The following suggestions will assist in supporting this perspective:

- Consider learning and assessment in a holistic way, acknowledging that each student will find identity, meaning, and purpose through connections to the community, to the natural world, and to values such as respect and gratitude.

- Incorporate family and community in learning and assessment. Include parents/caregivers, siblings, grandparents, aunts and uncles, and cousins. Also include community members, such as Elders, Knowledge Keepers, daycare staff, babysitters, and coaches. For this purpose, a template is included for FAMILY AND COMMUNITY CONNECTIONS: ASSESSING TOGETHER, which is found on page 57. After any lesson or module, students can take home a copy of this template to complete with family or community members (with permission). This template can also be completed by students in pairs, to enhance the sense of community in the classroom.

- Have students take home one of their self-assessment templates (STUDENT SELF-ASSESSMENT, STUDENT REFLECTIONS, SCIENCE JOURNAL, CORE COMPETENCY SELF-REFLECTION FRAMES, CORE COMPETENCY STUDENT REFLECTIONS: MODULE SUMMARY, or COOPERATIVE SKILLS SELF-ASSESSMENT) to explain it to a family or community member. These templates can also be shared with a peer to enhance the sense of community within the school.

Connecting Assessment to Curricular Competencies

Throughout *Hands-On Science*, suggestions are provided for student self-assessment, formative assessment, and summative assessment. Many of these suggestions are linked to the Curricular Competencies, as in the following example that focuses on Communication:

Formative Assessment

- Photograph students as they journal, to collect evidence of learning activities. Be sure to document student thinking after journaling. For example, meet with them individually to have them share their thoughts about the journaling experience and what they recorded in their journal. Use photographs taken as they journal to inspire reflection. Focus on students' ability to express and reflect on personal experiences of place. Use the INDIVIDUAL STUDENT OBSERVATIONS template on page 51 to record interview highlights.

The *Hands-On Science* Assessment Plan

This feature of the *Hands-On Science* Assessment Plan supports teachers in making connections between assessment strategies and the Curricular Connections focused upon at the kindergarten to grade-two levels.

Module Assessment Summary

At the end of each module, suggestions are provided for a summary of assessment. This includes:

- Collecting student work in a portfolio, so students can examine and discuss these artifacts of learning during a conference.
- Having students take home a copy of the FAMILY AND COMMUNITY CONNECTIONS: ASSESSING TOGETHER template on page 57 to complete with a family or community member.
- Having students complete the CORE COMPETENCY STUDENT REFLECTIONS: MODULE SUMMARY template, on page 48, to reflect on their use of the Core Competencies throughout the module and to determine next steps in their learning.
- Reviewing assessment templates completed by students and teachers throughout the module.

Important Note to Teachers

It is important to keep in mind that the ideas provided in *Hands-On Science* for student self-assessment, formative assessment, and summative assessment are merely suggestions. Teachers are encouraged to use the assessment strategies presented in a wide variety of ways, and to ensure that they build an effective assessment plan using these assessment ideas, as well as their own valuable experiences as educators.

References

British Columbia Ministry of Education. *A Framework for Classroom Assessment*. <https://curriculum.gov.bc.ca/sites/curriculum.gov.bc.ca/files/pdf/assessment/a-framework-for-classroom-assessment.pdf>

British Columbia Ministry of Education. *B.C. Performance Standards*. <https://www2.gov.bc.ca/gov/content/education-training/k-12/teach/bc-performance-standards>

British Columbia Ministry of Education. *BC's New Curriculum.* 2016. <https://curriculum.gov.bc.ca/>

British Columbia Ministry of Education. *Supporting the Self-Assessment and Reporting of Core Competencies*, 2016 <https://curriculum.gov.bc.ca/sites/curriculum.gov.bc.ca/files/pdf/supporting-self-assessment.pdf>.

Cameron, Caren, and Kathleen Gregory. *Rethinking Letter Grades: A Five-Step Approach for Aligning Letter Grades to Learning Standards*. Winnipeg: Portage & Main Press, 2014.

Davies, Anne. *Making Classroom Assessment Work* (3rd ed.). Courtenay, BC: Connections Publishing, 2011.

Manitoba Education. *Rethinking Classroom Assessment with Purpose in Mind: Assessment for Learning, Assessment as Learning, Assessment of Learning*, 2006.

Ontario Ministry of Education. *Growing Success: Assessment, Evaluation, and Reporting in Ontario Schools*, 2010. <www.edu.gov.on.ca/>.

Toulouse, Pamela. *Achieving Aboriginal Student Success*. Winnipeg: Portage & Main Press, 2011.

Date: _____   Name: _____

Student Self-Assessment
Looking at My Science Learning

1. Today in science, I _____
   _____
   _____

2. In science, I learned _____
   _____
   _____

3. I did very well at _____
   _____
   _____

4. One science skill that I am working on is _____
   _____
   _____

5. I would like to learn more about _____
   _____
   _____

6. One thing I like about science is _____
   _____
   _____

Note: The student may complete this self-assessment or the teacher can scribe for the student.

Date: _____ Name: _____

Student Reflections

| What I Did | What I Learned |
|---|---|//

Next Steps in My Learning	My Strengths and Challenges

Science Journal

Name: _____ Date: _____

Today, I _____

I learned _____

I would like to learn more about _____

Science Journal

Name: _____ Date: _____

Today, I _____

I learned _____

I would like to learn more about _____

Core Competency Discussion Prompts
Communication

Facet	I Can...
A. Connect and engage with others (to share and develop ideas)	■ ask questions ■ answer questions ■ be an active listener (My eyes are on the speaker. I show that I am interested in what they are saying.) ■ see that my classmates and I can sometimes have different ways to do things, see things, and understand things ■ use a calm voice when I disagree with others
B. Acquire, interpret, and present information (includes inquiries)	■ understand and share information about a topic that is important to me ■ present information clearly and in an organized way ■ present information and ideas to an audience I may not know
C. Collaborate to plan, carry out, and review constructions and activities	■ work with others; I do my share of my group's job ■ take on roles and responsibilities in a group ■ describe ideas ■ explain the ways my group agrees with our ideas
D. Explain/recount and reflect on experiences and accomplishments	■ give feedback to my classmates ■ listen to feedback from my classmates ■ use feedback from my classmates to make changes to my ideas ■ share simple experiences and activities and tell something I learned ■ show my learning ■ tell how my learning is connected to my experiences and hard work

Core Competency Discussion Prompts
Thinking: Critical Thinking

Facet	I Can...
A. Analyze and critique	<ul><li>show if I like something or not</li><li>use criteria</li><li>look at results from different points of view</li><li>reflect on and evaluate my thinking, products, and actions</li><li>think about my own beliefs and consider views that do not fit with them</li></ul>
B. Question and investigate	<ul><li>explore materials and actions</li><li>ask questions that have more than one answer</li><li>gather information</li><li>carefully think about different ways to solve a problem</li><li>decide if my sources of information are dependable</li><li>tell the difference between facts and opinions</li></ul>
C. Develop and design	<ul><li>experiment with different ways of doing things</li><li>help create criteria for design projects</li><li>keep track of my progress</li><li>change my actions to make sure I reach my goal</li><li>make choices that will help me meet my goals</li></ul>

Core Competency Discussion Prompts
Thinking: Creative Thinking

Facet	I Can...
A. **Novelty and value**	<ul><li>get ideas when I play (My ideas are fun for me and make me happy.)</li><li>get new ideas or build on other people's ideas, to create new things</li><li>think of new ideas as I follow my interests</li><li>think of ideas that are new to my classmates</li><li>make creative projects in an area that interests me</li></ul>
B. **Generating ideas**	<ul><li>get ideas when I use my senses to explore</li><li>build on others' ideas</li><li>add new ideas of my own to create new things</li><li>add new ideas of my own to solve problems</li><li>learn a lot about something (e.g., by doing research, talking to others, practising), so I can create new ideas</li><li>calm my mind (e.g., walking away for a while, doing something relaxing, being playful), so I can be more creative</li><li>have interests that I continue for a long time</li></ul>
C. **Developing ideas**	<ul><li>make my ideas work or change what I am doing</li><li>usually make my ideas work with materials if I keep playing with them</li><li>learn and use the skills I need to make my ideas work, and usually succeed, even if it takes a few tries</li><li>use my experiences for future learning</li><li>try to develop my ideas over a long period of time</li></ul>

Core Competency Discussion Prompts
Personal and Social: Positive Personal & Cultural Identity

Facet	I Can...
A. **Relationships and cultural contexts**	<ul><li>describe my family</li><li>describe my community</li><li>tell about the different groups that I belong to</li><li>understand that my identity is made up of life experiences, family history, heritage, and peer groups</li><li>understand that learning is forever, and I will continue to grow as a person</li></ul>
B. **Personal values and choices**	<ul><li>tell what is important to me</li><li>explain my values and how they affect choices I make</li><li>tell how some important parts of my life have influenced my values</li><li>understand how my values affect my choices</li></ul>
C. **Personal strengths and abilities**	<ul><li>describe my characteristics</li><li>describe my talents and the things I do well</li><li>think about the things I do well</li><li>describe how I am a leader in my community</li><li>understand that I will continue to develop new strengths and skills to help me meet new challenges</li></ul>

Core Competency Discussion Prompts
Personal and Social: Personal Awareness and Responsibility

Facet	I Can...
A. Self-determination	<ul><li>be happy and proud of how well I did</li><li>celebrate my hard work and success</li><li>believe in myself</li><li>believe in my ideas</li><li>imagine and work toward change in myself and the world</li><li>learn about things in which people have different opinions</li></ul>
B. Self-regulation	<ul><li>sometimes name different emotions</li><li>use strategies that help me manage my feelings and emotions</li><li>work through hard tasks</li><li>make a plan and evaluate the results</li><li>take responsibility for my goals</li><li>take responsibility for my own learning</li><li>take responsibility for my own behaviour</li></ul>
C. Well-being	<ul><li>participate in activities that are healthy for my mind and body</li><li>tell/show how these healthy activities help me</li><li>take some responsibility for caring for my own body and mind</li><li>make choices that are good for my mind and body and keep me safe in my community, including my online conversations with others</li><li>use strategies to find peace when I am feeling stress</li><li>live a healthy life that includes both work and play</li></ul>

Date: _____   Name: _____

Core Competency Self-Reflection Frame
Communication

I Can…	Examples	Next Steps
I can answer questions.		
I can listen to others when they speak.		
I can share my learning.		
I can work in a group.		

Date: _____ Name: _____

Core Competency Self-Reflection Frame
Creative Thinking

- I can learn a lot through play.
- I can get new ideas as I learn.
- I can learn new skills as I try out my ideas.
- I can make my ideas work.

One thing that I would like to work on is _____

Name: _____

Date: _____

Core Competency Self-Reflection Frame
Critical Thinking

- I can explore materials.
- I can experiment with different ways of doing things.
- I can show if I like something or not.
- I can ask questions and gather information.

One goal that I have is _____

45

Date: _____ Name: _____

Core Competency Self-Reflection Frame
Positive Personal and Cultural Identity

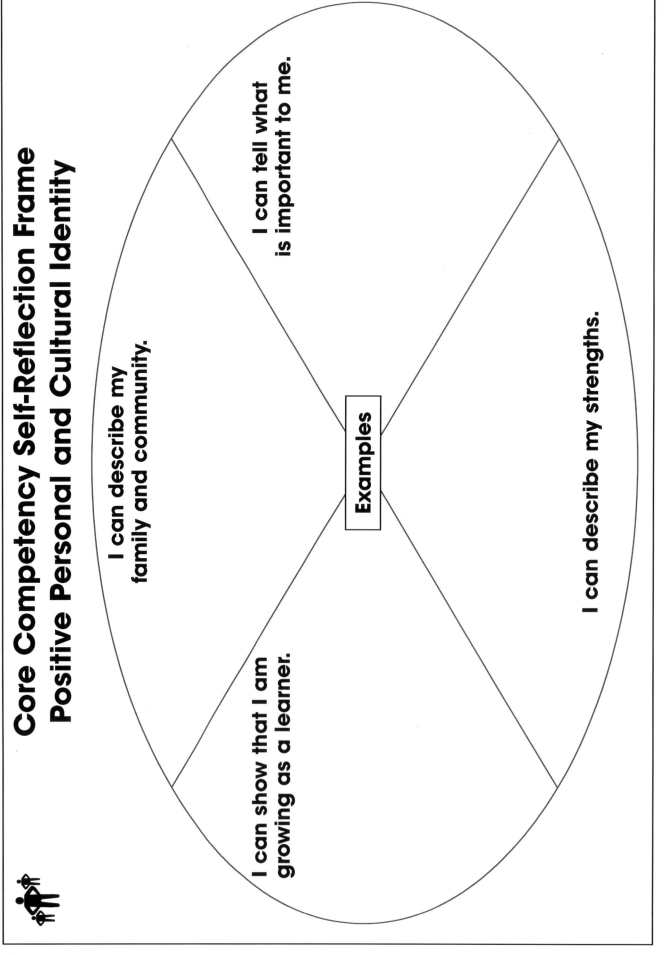

- I can tell what is important to me.
- I can describe my family and community.
- I can describe my strengths.
- I can show that I am growing as a learner.

Examples

Date: _____ Name: _____

Core Competency Self-Reflection Frame
Personal Awareness and Responsibility

I can be proud when I have done well.

I can describe my feelings.

I can work hard to finish a job.

I can make choices that make me feel good and stay safe.

Date: _____ Name: _____

Core Competency Student Reflections

Module Summary

Core Competency: _____

What I Did

Next Steps

Date: _____   Name: _____

Cooperative Skills Self-Assessment

Students in my group:

_____   _____

_____   _____

Group Work—How Did I Do Today?

Group Work	How I Did (✓)		
	🌰	🌱	🌻
I shared ideas.			
I listened to others.			
I asked questions.			
I encouraged others.			
I helped with the work.			
I stayed on task.			

I did very well at _____

_____

Next time, I would like to do better at _____

_____

Anecdotal Record

Purpose of Observation: _____

Student/Group	**Date**	**Student/Group**	**Date**
Comments		**Comments**	
Student/Group	**Date**	**Student/Group**	**Date**
Comments		**Comments**	
Student/Group	**Date**	**Student/Group**	**Date**
Comments		**Comments**	

Individual Student Observations

Purpose of Observation: _____

Student:	**Date:**

Observations:

Student:	**Date:**

Observations:

Student:	**Date:**

Observations:

Cooperative Skills Teacher Assessment

Date: _____ Task: _____

Group Member	Cooperative Skills				
	Contributes ideas and questions	Respects and accepts contributions of others	Negotiates roles and responsibilities of each group member	Remains focused and encourages others to stay on task	Completes individual commitment to the group

Rubric

Activity: _____

Module: _____

Date: _____

E – Emerging
D – Developing
P – Proficient
EX – Extending

Student	Criteria				

Sample Rubric

Activity: Looking at Seeds

Module: Living Things

Date: _____

		E – Emerging
		D – Developing
		P – Proficient
		EX – Extending

Criteria

Student	Observes Seeds Carefully	Asks Questions About the Seeds	Sorts Seeds and Gives Sorting Rules	Describes Seeds in Detail						
Jarod	P	P	D	P						
Aisha	P	D	P	D						

Name: _____

Portfolio Table of Contents

Entry **Date** **Selection**

1. _____ _____
2. _____ _____
3. _____ _____
4. _____ _____
5. _____ _____
6. _____ _____
7. _____ _____
8. _____ _____
9. _____ _____
10. _____ _____
11. _____ _____
12. _____ _____
13. _____ _____
14. _____ _____
15. _____ _____
16. _____ _____
17. _____ _____
18. _____ _____
19. _____ _____
20. _____ _____

Date: _____   Name: _____

Portfolio Entry Record

This work was chosen by _____

This work is _____

_____

I chose this work because _____

_____

_____

_____

_____

Note: The student may complete this form or the teacher can scribe for the student.

✂- ✂

Date: _____   Name: _____

Portfolio Entry Record

This work was chosen by _____

This work is _____

_____

I chose this work because _____

_____

_____

_____

_____

Note: The student may complete this form or the teacher can scribe for the student.

Date: _____ Name: _____

Family and Community Connections: Assessing Together

Family/Community Member's Name: _____

Draw a picture that shows what you have been learning in science. Work together to label your picture and describe your learning in words.

_____
_____
_____

What do you like best about what you have been learning in science?

_____
_____
_____

What does your family/community member like best about what you have been learning in science?

_____
_____
_____

What Are the Properties of Matter?

About This Module

This module of **Hands-On Science** focuses on the properties of matter. Students will be introduced to the properties of solids, liquids, and gases as three states of matter. They will conduct investigations that explore the following Big Ideas:

- Humans interact with matter every day through familiar materials.
- Matter is useful because of its properties.
- Materials can be changed through physical and chemical processes.

While investigating these Big Ideas, the Curricular Competencies will be addressed as students use the following skills, strategies, and processes:

QP	questioning and predicting
PC	planning and conducting investigations
PA	processing and analyzing data and information
AI	applying and innovating
C	communicating
E	evaluating

See the Curricular Competencies Correlation Chart, page 65, for more information.

Matter is anything that takes up space and has weight. Everything in our world is matter. We are surrounded by objects made of matter or, more specifically, objects that are made of different materials. Colour, odour, taste, weight, and hardness (rigidity) are physical properties of matter.

Incorporate Indigenous perspectives and worldviews into lessons whenever possible. This module provides many opportunities for students to learn about the ways Indigenous peoples view the world. By understanding characteristics of objects and materials in nature, Indigenous peoples are able to use these resources for many things, including:

- wood for building shelters
- fur for making warm clothing
- animal hides for waterproof material
- rocks and stones for making tools
- clay for making pottery

Indigenous peoples also understand the importance of limiting waste. As an example, all parts of hunted animals are used, and nothing is wasted. This respect for natural resources is a precursor to the present-day principle of *Reduce, Reuse,* and *Recycle*. However, there is more to it:

> The interaction that Indigenous peoples have with the environment is our law. It is a way of understanding the world, a way of living in interdependence with our community. These are cultural practices. These are spiritual beliefs. We have to show respect for, and honour the spirit of the animal. For example, if we are disrespectful to Salmon or to Deer, next time we are hungry, we may not see them again. (When we talk about the spirit of the animal, we capitalize, and we leave out any articles. So we do not say "the salmon" we say "Salmon" when talking about the spirit of the animal). We are connected to our resources spiritually, and if we are being disrespectful, we will not have access to resources, or we will have access in a different way, perhaps lessened, or in an unhealthy way. (Melanie Nelson, Indigenous Consultant)

Indigenous teachings about the properties of matter, including the characteristics of solids, liquids, and gases, focus not only on the ▶

properties of each state but also on how each can affect daily life (e.g., water contributing to life, air and wind, the properties of solid materials used for survival as in shelter and clothing).

When implementing place-based learning, there are many opportunities to consider Indigenous perspectives and knowledge. Outdoor learning provides an excellent opportunity to identify the importance of place. For example, use a map of the local area to have students identify where the learning location is in relation to the school. This will help students develop a stronger image of their community and the surrounding area.

Identify on whose traditional territory the school is located, as well as the traditional territory of the location for any place-based learning. The following map, "First Nations in British Columbia," from Indigenous Services Canada can be used for this purpose: <www.aadnc-aandc.gc.ca/DAM/DAM-INTER-BC/STAGING/texte-text/inacmp_1100100021016_eng.pdf>.

Incorporate land acknowledgment when students have learned on whose territory the school and the place-based learning location are located. The following example can be used for guidance:

- We would like to acknowledge that we are gathered today on the traditional, ancestral, and unceded territory of the _____ people.

NOTE: Many school districts have established protocols for land acknowledgment. Check with colleagues who support Indigenous education to see if there are specific protocols to follow.

Planning Tips for Teachers

- Collect a variety of materials and objects for observation in the classroom:
    - plastics (e.g., cups, spoons, bags, empty pop bottles, jugs, food containers)
    - metals (e.g., spoons, paper clips, nails, screws, aluminum foil)
    - rubber (e.g., balls, erasers, balloons)
    - cloth (e.g., cotton, rayon, linen, nylon, flannel, leather)
    - wood (e.g., pencils, blocks, wooden spoons)
    - natural objects (e.g., branches, rocks, shells, feathers, fur)
- Collect a variety of visuals. Include images of building materials (e.g., lumber, shingles, concrete, gravel, insulation, glass, metal), household objects (e.g., appliances, furniture, cooking tools), and personal items (e.g., clothing, shoes, purses, jewellery).
- Contact local Elders and Knowledge Keepers to share stories and knowledge related to lesson topics. Please see Indigenous Perspectives and Knowledge, page 33, for considerations when inviting Elders and Knowledge Keepers to speak to students.
- Gather a variety of reading materials at a range of reading levels appropriate for your class. Include fiction and nonfiction resources. Collect high-quality books with detailed illustrations and photographs to pique students' interests about properties of matter. These books may be used at the learning centre, the Makerspace centre, or for general reference throughout the module. Please see Resources for Students on page 67 for suggestions.
- Preview and bookmark websites students may use during the module.
- Have students make place-based journals for use throughout the module. These can be made from notebooks with sturdy covers or simply drawing paper and clipboards. Use a zipper-lock plastic bag to carry journal supplies (e.g., pencils, sharpeners, pencil crayons [rather than markers which will bleed if wet], stretch gloves for journaling on cooler days).
- Be sure to keep all charts and displays created during each lesson, as well as all completed student work. These may be referred to again in subsequent lessons. All charts and other materials are used in the

concluding lesson, which is a final inquiry project.
- Record the guided inquiry question for each lesson (e.g., on a sentence strip) for display throughout related investigations.

Loose Parts

Create Loose Parts bins to explore objects and materials. Fill bins with various objects and materials, such as:

- thread spools
- metal objects (e.g., paper clips, nuts, bolts, washers)
- wooden objects (e.g., blocks, sticks, tree slices, craft sticks)
- fabric swatches, felt, faux fur
- seeds and pine cones
- shells
- rocks
- glass and plastic beads
- jar lids

Loose Parts bins encourage personalized learning, as students can select bins to explore. Offer provocations to inspire students (e.g., How can you use Loose Parts to show how matter is important in your life?). Loose Parts can also expand inquiry. For example, students might explore a bin of shells and then choose to initiate an inquiry to find out the origin of various shells in the collection.

Makerspace

Develop a Makerspace centre. Classroom Makerspaces are usually designed as centres where students learn together and collaborate on do-it-yourself projects. Students are given the opportunity to work with a variety of age-appropriate tools, as well as with everyday, arts-and-crafts, and recycled materials.

Set up a Makerspace centre in your classroom that encourages informal learning about the properties of matter. Collect a variety of materials and equipment that reflect the challenges students might take on at the centre. Include general materials, such as those listed in the Introduction to **Hands-On Science** (page 19), as well as module-specific materials. For this module, include a variety of materials (e.g., wood, recycled plastic and cardboard, modelling clay), natural items (e.g., branches, grasses, rocks, fur, feathers), as well as containers of liquids and tools to encourage investigation (e.g., measuring cups, funnels, siphons, eyedroppers, spray bottles, magnifying glasses).

SAFETY NOTE: Ensure all solids and liquids at the centre are safe for students to use. Also consider student allergies when selecting supplies for the centre. Engage in a discussion about safety and respect at the Makerspace centre with students before beginning this module. Consider small parts and potential hazards for students of all ages and abilities who will have access to the Makerspace centre. For kindergarten to grade-two students, exploration needs to be supervised.

Do-it-yourself projects may include anything related to the concepts of properties of matter. Projects students might initiate include (but are not limited to):

- designing and building a model of a structure
- designing and constructing a useful device
- creating a collage made with various materials
- testing the strength of different objects or materials
- designing a device to clean water
- creating a new product/device out of recycled solids, to reuse those products and to prevent them from going to landfill
- designing and constructing devices that are buoyant in water, and testing these devices with coins or weights
- designing a container that can hold a solid, liquid, or gas

- creating a puppet play demonstrating the properties of solids, liquids, and gases
- creating public service announcements to bring attention to water issues

Literacy connections that might inspire projects include:

- *If I Built a House* by Chris Van Dusen
- *Twenty-One Elephants and Still Standing* by April Jones Prince
- *Dreaming Up: A Celebration of Building* by Christy Hale
- *Iggy Peck, Architect* by Andrea Beaty
- *Rosie Revere, Engineer* by Andrea Beaty
- *Ada Twist, Scientist* by Andrea Beaty
- *Sadie and the Snowman* by Allen Morgan
- *Water Can Be...* by Laura Purdie Salas
- *A Drop of Water: A Book of Science and Wonder* by Walter Wick
- *The Drop in My Drink: The Story of Water on Our Planet* by Meredith Hooper

As inquiry questions are posed within each lesson, you will find these questions inspire other do-it-yourself projects. Students may determine answers to these questions through the creating they do at the Makerspace centre. Remember to not direct learning here; simply create conditions for learning to happen.

Science Vocabulary

Throughout this module, teachers should use, and encourage students to use, vocabulary such as:

- *absorbent, air, characteristic, chemical change, cloth, compost, dissolve, dull, fabric, flexible, glass, join, liquid, mass/weight, material, metal, object, opaque, paper, physical change, plastic, property, recycle, reduce, reuse, rough, shiny, smooth, solid, structure, substance, texture, thick, thin, tool, translucent, transparent, viscosity, waste, waterproof, wood*

For this module, provide samples of materials (e.g., wood, metal, plastic, cloth) and use objects to demonstrate characteristics of matter (e.g., flexible, smooth, opaque). Visual and tactile cues enhance students' understanding of concepts and vocabulary.

Infuse vocabulary related to scientific inquiry skills into daily lessons. Display vocabulary in the classroom throughout the year, as it relates to all science Big Ideas. Have students brainstorm which skills they are being asked to use as they work in particular lessons. Discuss what the skill looks and sounds like as students explore and investigate. Vocabulary related to scientific inquiry skills include:

- *access, ask, brainstorm, collect, compare, connect, consider, construct, cooperate, create, describe, estimate, explain, explore, find, follow, graph, identify, improve, investigate, match, measure, observe, order, plan, predict, recognize, record, repeat, research, respond, select, sequence, test*

Early in the module, create a word wall on a bulletin board, on poster paper, or on chart paper. Record new vocabulary on the word wall as it is introduced. Place the word wall in a location where all students can see and refer to the words during activities and discussion. Have students work with the terms on a regular basis by creating their own definitions, giving examples, linking terms in sentences, and using terms in context.

NOTE: Include terminology in languages other than English, such as Indigenous languages, on the word wall. This is a way of acknowledging and respecting students' cultural backgrounds, while enhancing learning for all students. A variety of online dictionaries may be used as a source for translations. For example:

- <www.firstvoices.com/en/Halqemeylem>

Online dictionaries are also available for other languages that reflect the class cultural makeup.

Curriculum Learning Framework

	K	1	2
Big Idea	Humans interact with matter every day through familiar materials.	Matter is useful because of its properties.	Materials can be changed through physical and chemical processes.
Sample Guiding Inquiry Questions	■ What is matter? ■ How do you interact with matter? ■ What qualities do different forms of matter have? ■ Where is matter in our lives?	■ What makes the properties of matter useful? ■ How do the properties of materials help connect to the function of materials?	■ Why would we want to change the physical properties of an object? ■ What are some natural processes that involve chemical and physical changes?
Content	■ properties of familiar materials: colour, texture (smooth or rough), flexibility (bendable or stretchable), hardness, lustre (shiny or dull), absorbency, etc. [lesson 1, 2, 3, 4, 8, 14, 21] ■ Types of familiar materials: fabric, wood, plastic, glass, metal/foil, sand, etc. [lesson 1, 2, 3, 5, 8, 10, 21]	■ specific properties: solids keep shape; liquids and gases flow [lesson 1, 2, 3, 12, 13, 14, 15, 17, 21] ■ properties of materials allow us to use them in different ways [lesson 1, 2, 3, 6, 8, 9, 11, 21] ■ properties of local materials determine use by First Peoples (local examples: cedar for canoes, mountain goat horns used as spoons, etc.) [lesson 1, 2, 3, 6, 7, 9, 14, 16, 20, 21]	■ physical ways of changing materials: warming, cooling, cutting, bending, stirring, mixing [lesson 1, 2, 3, 18, 20, 21] ■ materials may be combined or physically changed to be used in different ways (e.g., plants can be ground up and combined with other materials to make dyes) [lesson 1, 2, 3, 7, 9, 10, 11, 15, 16, 20, 21] ■ chemical ways of changing materials: cooking, burning, etc. [lesson 1, 2, 3, 19, 20, 21]
Core Competencies	*Thinking* *Communicating* *Social and Personal*		

Curricular Competencies Correlation Chart

Throughout this module, students will develop Curricular Competencies by participating in learning experiences that focus on specific skills, strategies, and processes. The chart below represents the multiple opportunities students have to explore the Curricular Competencies.

Curricular Competencies	1	2	3	4	5	6	7	8	9	10	11	12	13	14	15	16	17	18	19	20	21
(QP) Questioning and Predicting																					
Demonstrate curiosity and a sense of wonder about the properties of matter.	√	√	√	√	√	√	√	√	√	√	√	√	√	√	√	√	√	√	√	√	√
Observe the properties of matter in familiar contexts.	√	√	√	√	√	√	√	√	√	√	√	√	√	√	√	√	√	√	√	√	√
Ask simple questions about the properties of matter.	√	√	√	√	√	√	√	√	√	√	√	√	√	√	√	√	√	√	√	√	√
Make simple predictions about the properties of matter.	√	√				√	√	√	√	√				√	√		√	√	√	√	
(PC) Planning and Conducting Investigations																					
Make exploratory observations using senses.	√	√	√	√	√	√	√	√	√	√	√	√	√	√	√	√	√	√	√	√	√
Record observations.	√	√	√	√		√	√	√	√	√	√	√		√	√	√	√	√	√		
Safely manipulate materials.	√	√	√	√	√	√	√	√	√	√	√	√	√	√	√	√	√	√	√	√	√
Make simple measurements using nonstandard units.				√			√			√				√							
(PA) Processing and Analyzing Data and Information																					
Experience and interpret the local environment.	√		√					√			√						√				
Recognize First Peoples stories (including oral and written narratives), songs, and art, as ways to share knowledge.	√	√	√	√		√	√	√	√	√	√	√		√	√	√	√	√	√		
Discuss observations about the properties of matter.	√	√	√	√	√	√	√	√	√	√	√	√	√	√	√	√	√	√	√	√	√
Represent observations and ideas by drawing charts and simple pictographs.				√		√	√	√	√	√		√	√	√		√		√		√	
Sort and classify data and information using drawings, pictographs, and provided tables.	√		√	√	√		√		√		√			√							
Compare observations with predictions through discussion.	√	√				√	√							√	√		√	√	√	√	
Identify simple patterns and connections related to the properties of matter.									√								√				

Properties of Matter for Grades K–2

Curricular Competencies	1	2	3	4	5	6	7	8	9	10	11	12	13	14	15	16	17	18	19	20	21
(AI) Applying and Innovating																					
Take part in caring for self, family, classroom, and school through personal approaches.										√	√									√	
Transfer and apply learning to new situations.										√				√	√	√					
Generate and introduce new or refined ideas when problem solving.	√	√	√	√	√	√	√	√	√	√	√	√	√	√	√	√	√	√	√	√	√
(C) Communicating																					
Share observations and ideas orally, or through written language, drawing, or role-play.	√	√	√	√	√	√	√	√	√	√	√	√	√	√	√	√	√	√	√	√	√
Express and reflect on personal experiences of place.	√																				
(E) Evaluating																					
Compare observations of the properties of matter with those of others.	√	√	√	√	√	√	√	√	√	√	√	√	√	√	√	√	√	√	√	√	√
Consider some environmental consequences of their actions as related to the properties of matter.	√		√		√	√	√			√											

Resources for Students

NOTE: Resources marked with an asterisk are considered to be authentic resources, meaning that they reference the Indigenous community they came from, they state the individual that shared the story and gave permission for the story to be used publicly, and the person who originally shared the story is Indigenous. Stories that are works of fiction were written by an Indigenous author. For more information, please see *Authentic First Peoples Resources* at: <www.fnesc.ca/learningfirstpeoples/>.

Books

*Aleck, Celestine. *Taking Care of Our Mother Earth*. Nanaimo, BC: Strong Nations, 2016.

Alperin, Mara. *Goldilocks and the Three Bears*. London: Little Tiger Press, 2014.

*Argueta, Jorge. *Talking With Mother Earth*. Toronto: House of Anansi, 2016.

*Avingaq, Susan, and Vestula Maren. *Fishing With Grandma*. Iqaluit, NU: Inhabit Media, 2016.

Beaty, Andrea. *Ada Twist, Scientist*. New York: Abrams Books for Young Readers, 2016.

Beaty, Andrea. *Iggy Peck, Architect*. New York: Abrams Books for Young Readers, 2007. (also available in French)

Beaty, Andrea. *Rosie Revere, Engineer*. New York: Abrams Books for Young Readers, 2013. (also available in French)

Boreham, Brenda. *We Are All Connected: The Earth, Our Home*. Nanaimo, BC: Strong Nations, 2017.

Boreham, Brenda. *We Are All Connected: The Earth, We Share*. Nanaimo, BC: Strong Nations, 2017.

Bunting, Eve. *Ducky*. New York: Clarion Books, 1997.

Carney, Margaret. *At Grandpa's Sugar Bush*. Toronto: Kids Can Press, 1997.

Crook, Connie Brummel. *Maple Moon*. Markham, ON: Fitzhenry and Whiteside, 1999.

Delmege, Sarah (retold). *Goldilocks and the Three Bears*. New York: Parragon, 2012.

*Flaherty, Louise. *Things That Keep Us Warm*. Toronto: Inhabit Education, 2016.

Hale, Christy. *Dreaming Up: A Celebration of Building*. New York: Lee & Low Books, 2012.

Hill, Tad. *Duck and Goose*. Toronto: Schwartz & Wade, 2006.

*Holloway, Pam. *Counting to 100 in the Bighouse*. Campbell River, BC: Cedar Moon Creations, 2015.

*Holloway, Pam. *Little Ceder, Big Cedar*. Campbell River, BC: Cedar Moon Creations, 2015.

Hooper, Meredith. *The Drop in My Drink: The Story of Water on Our Planet*. London: Lincoln Children's Books, 2015.

*Hunt, Dallas. *Awâsis and the World-Famous Bannock*. Winnipeg, MB: HighWater Press, 2018.

Keats, Ezra Jack. *The Snowy Day*. New York: Viking Books for Young Readers, 1996.

Laverde, Arlene. *Alaska's Three Little Pigs*. New York: Random House, 2015.

Linton, Marilyn. *The Maple Syrup Book*. Toronto: Kids Can Press, 1993.

Litwin, Eric. *Pete the Cat: I Love My White Shoes*. New York: HarperCollins, 2010.

*McLellan, Joe. *Nanabosho Steals Fire*. Winnipeg, MB: Pemmican, 2009.

*McLeod, Elaine. *Lessons From Mother Earth.* Toronto: Groundwood Books, 2010.

Milbourne, Anna. *The Rainy Day.* Newmarket, ON: Usborne Books, 2012.

Morgan, Allen. *Sadie and the Snowman.* Toronto: Kids Can Press, 1985.

Munsch, Robert. *Mud Puddle.* Toronto: Annick Press, 2012.

Prince, April Jones. *Twenty-One Elephants and Still Standing.* Boston, MA: HMH Books for Young Readers, 2005.

Rustad, Martha. *Why Do Puddles Disappear?* Minneapolis: Lerner Publication Group, 2015.

Salas, Laura Purdie. *Water Can Be....* Minneapolis: Millbrook Press, 2014.

Scieszka, Jon. *The True Story of the Three Little Pigs.* New York: Random House, 2017.

Teague, Mark. *The Three Little Pigs and the Somewhat Bad Wolf.* New York: Scholastic, 2013.

*The Sechelt Nation. *How the Robin Got Its Red Breast.* Vancouver: Harbour Publishing, 2003.

*The Sechelt Nation. *Ch'askin: A Legend of the Sechelt People.* Vancouver: Harbour Publishing, 2003.

Van Dusen, Chris. *If I Built a House.* New York: Dial Books for Young Readers, 2012.

*Vickers, Roy Henry and Robert Budd. *Cloudwalker.* Vancouver: Harbour Publishing, 2014.

*Wheeler, Bernelda. *I Can't Have Bannock but the Beaver Has a Dam.* Winnipeg, MB: HighWater Press, 2016.

Wick, Walter. *A Drop of Water: A Book of Science and Wonder.* New York: Scholastic Press, 1997.

*Yahgulanaas, Michael. *The Little Hummingbird.* Vancouver: Greystone Books, 2010.

Websites

- **www.bbc.co.uk/schools/scienceclips/ages/7_8/science_7_8.shtml**
  BBC Schools—Characteristics of Materials: Game that allows users to test if materials are waterproof, flexible, transparent, or strong.

- **www.bbc.co.uk/schools/scienceclips/ages/6_7/science_6_7.shtml**
  BBC Schools—Grouping and Changing Materials: Game for sorting objects based on their materials.

- **www.bbc.co.uk/schools/scienceclips/ages/5_6/science_5_6.shtml**
  BBC Schools—Sorting and Using Materials: Game that allows users to test if materials are waterproof or bendable (or both, or neither).

- **www.learningscience.org/psc1apropofmaterials.htm**
  LearningScience.Org—Properties of Objects and Materials (K–4): Variety of activities for students to explore the characteristics of objects and materials.

- **www.sciencekids.co.nz/gamesactivities/materialproperties.html**
  Science Kids—Science Games for Kids—Properties of Materials: Students can learn about the properties of materials (are they flexible, waterproof, strong, or transparent?) as they experiment with various objects.

- **exchange.smarttech.com**
  SMART Exchange: Use the search bar with key terms (e.g., materials) to find appropriate activities for your class.

▶

- **https://umistapotlatch.ca/enseignants-education/cours_9-lesson_9-eng.php**
  "Materials: Traditional Dyes"—Living Tradition: The Kwakwaka'wakw Potlatch on the Northwest Coast: This lesson plan includes information, photographs, and videos related to how Indigenous peoples, particularly the Kwakwaka'wakw, extract dyes from natural sources.

- **https://scientistinresidence.ca/science-lesson-plans/soils-plants-and-first-nations/**
  "Soils, Plants, and First Nations"—Life Science Lessons: The lesson plan "First Nations Plants and Their Uses" provides background information and uses for various local plants, including those used to create natural dyes.

- **www.indiana.edu/~bobweb/Handout/d1.uses.htm**
  Creativity Test—Guilford's Alternative Uses Task: Shows an example of an activity to encourage students to come up with alternative uses for everyday objects.

- **www.kapili.com/chem4kids/**
  Rader's Chem4Kids.com: Designed for teachers and students studying matter (solids, liquids, gases, and plasmas) and its physical properties, states, and phases. Includes a periodic table the elements.

- **classroom.jc-schools.net/sci-units/matter.htm**
  Science Online: Provides skills, lesson plans, and interactive science activities for elementary grades, and includes a section on matter.

- **https://www.stevespanglerscience.com/lab/experiments/seven-layer-density-column**
  Seven Layer Density Column—Steve Spangler Science: The procedure for making Seven Layer Density Column, a stack of seven different liquids in seven layers.

- **https://www.thoughtco.com/the-history-of-silly-putty-1779330**
  The History of Silly Putty—A short history and invention of Silly Putty, including some fun facts about the product.

- **www.sciencekids.co.nz/**
  Science Kids offers science videos, experiments, science-fair ideas, a science photo library, online games, and a facts page full of essential science information.

Videos

- **https://www.youtube.com/watch?v=IAf_iVuZ-vU&list=PLtXf78zN40CJQd64pimo5EcGdIvEnbYFs&index=2**
  "Robot Separates Recyclables from Other Garbage." NTDTV (2:52).

NOTE: This valuable video focuses on building Applied Design, Skills, and Technologies, as students analyze the robot as a prototype. Ask students to identify properties that the robot can detect, to compare the efficiency of such a machine to human workers, and to propose improvements to the design of the robot.

- **https://www.youtube.com/watch?v=TjnNOCbuoCA**
  "The 3 R's for Kids." Smart Learning for All. Animated video (10:04).

- **https://www.youtube.com/watch?v=wll8HXa3HLk**
  "Reading Rainbow How Trash Is Recycled with LeVar Burton." Tara Aperauch (6:23).

- **https://www.youtube.com/watch?v=BaFpv03hq-4**
  "Recycle." WonderGroveKids. Animated video (3:06).

- https://www.youtube.com/watch?v=7SrdKlzvHSs
  "How to Make Maple Syrup." Quad Squad (6:24).
- https://www.youtube.com/watch?v=R-x5QOSqP3E
  "How To Build An Igloo | A Boy Among Polar Bears | BBC." BBC Worldwide (2:53).
- https://www.youtube.com/watch?v=Ptjl9dEKZjs
  "Maple Syrup Production." Ontario Maple Syrup Producers' Association (8:05).
- https://www.youtube.com/watch?v=flaT5SoSSRg
  "Kleekhoot Gold Bigleaf Maple Syrup." Hupacasath First Nation (3:05).
- https://vancouverisland.ctvnews.ca/sweet-success-b-c-first-nation-launches-commercial-maple-syrup-venture-1.3318912
  "Sweet success: B.C. First Nation launches commercial maple syrup venture." CTV Vancouver Island (2:10).
- https://www.youtube.com/watch?v=n6wpNhyreDE
  "The chemistry of cookies—Stephanie Warren." Ted-Ed (4:25).
- https://www.youtube.com/watch?v=oxPaD_2K_08
  "Tapping Into The Science Of The Maple Sugar Harvest." CBCSaskatchewan (1:00).
- https://www.youtube.com/watch?v=H3PxZfJPrpE
  "Air Occupies Space - Elementary Science." Elearning (1:19).
- https://www.youtube.com/watch?v=xh1-Ynl6Z_Q
  "Air contains oxygen experiment - Elementary Science." Elearnin (1:23).
- https://www.youtube.com/watch?v=ncORPosDrjl
  "The Water Cycle | The Dr. Binocs Show | Learn Videos For Kids." Peekaboo Kidz (3:08).
- https://www.imaginationstationtoledo.org/educator/activities/how-to-make-a-naked-egg
  "How to make a Naked Egg?" ISTscience (3:27).

1 Initiating Event: What Do We Observe, Think, and Wonder About Objects and Materials in Nature?

Information for Teachers

In this lesson, students will participate in place-based learning to explore objects and materials in a local natural environment. Focus on objects found in this area, both natural and human-made, as well as the materials from which these objects are made. Plan ahead to select a location and encourage students to suggest local natural areas.

If possible, invite a local Elder or Knowledge Keeper to share relevant stories, as well as knowledge of the land—its features, and the objects and materials found there.

NOTE: See Indigenous Perspectives and Knowledge, page 33, for guidelines for inviting Elders and Knowledge Keepers to speak to students.

To prepare for exploring nature with students, refer to *A Place for Wonder: Reading and Writing Nonfiction in the Primary Grades*, by Georgia Heard and Jennifer McDonough.

Materials

- digital cameras
- magnifying glasses
- tweezers
- stretch gloves
- string
- paper plates
- garden tools (e.g., shovels, forks)
- portable whiteboard (optional)
- whiteboard markers (optional)
- chart paper (with a sturdy backboard)
- markers
- map of local area
- map of traditional territories of First Peoples in British Columbia (see Engage)
- pails
- objects collected during the nature walk (e.g., seeds, nuts, twigs, leaves, rocks, shells)
- ledger-sized paper
- crayons
- computer/tablet with internet access
- place-based journals and supplies (see page 61)
- Learning-Centre Task Card A: How Can I Sort Objects From Nature? (2.1.1)
- Learning-Centre Task Card B: Counting Loose Parts (2.1.2).

Engage

Explain to students that they will be exploring a natural environment through a nature walk. Discuss the location for this place-based learning. Ask:

- Who has been to this place before?
- How did you get there?
- What is it like there?
- What do you think we will see there? Smell? Hear? Feel?
- What kinds of living things might we see?
- What kinds of nonliving things might we see?

Have students share their background knowledge, predictions, inferences, and ideas about the natural environment they will visit, and the objects they might investigate there. Record their ideas on chart paper. Later, students can refer back to their ideas to see how their thinking changes.

Have students share with a partner what they are most excited about in visiting this location.

To help students develop a stronger image of their community and surrounding area, use a map of the local area to identify where the place-based learning location is in relation to the school. This is an excellent opportunity to identify the importance of place.

Identify on whose traditional territory the school is located, as well as the traditional territory of the location for the place-based learning (if different). The following map, "First Nations in British Columbia," from Indigenous Services Canada can be used for this purpose: <www.aadnc-aandc.gc.ca/DAM/DAM-INTER-BC/STAGING/texte-text/inacmp_1100100021016_eng.pdf>.

This activity ties into the First Peoples Principles of Learning related to sense of place.

Incorporate land acknowledgment when students have learned on whose territory the school and place-based learning location are located. The following example can be used for guidance:

- We would like to acknowledge that we are gathered today on the traditional, ancestral, and unceded territory of the _____ people.

NOTE: Many school districts have established protocols for land acknowledgment. Check with colleagues who support Indigenous education to see if there are specific protocols to follow.

Review any other protocols for field trips, providing students with opportunities to ask questions and clarify expectations.

 SAFETY NOTE: Remind students never to taste anything without permission. Review other safety considerations, such as plants that may cause skin irritations and bodies of water that may be present at the place-based learning location. Also be aware of students' allergies during the activity.

Discuss with students the importance of respecting nature. Have them brainstorm ways in which they can demonstrate this. Create an anchor chart on chart paper to display in the classroom. This can be reviewed each time students go outside to visit a natural environment. For example:

- Be respectful of all living things.
- Never break off branches from trees or pick wildflowers.
- Collect only a few objects to take back to the classroom.
- Always clean up after ourselves.

Introduce the guided inquiry question: **What do we observe, think, and wonder about objects and materials in nature?**

Explore Part One

NOTE: The activities in this section connect to the First Peoples Principles of Learning related to supporting the well-being of the land and recognizing the consequences of one's actions. Be sure to connect consequences to the place-based learning locations already visited during the module. For example, discuss how a specific natural environment would change if the trees were cut down to build houses.

When the class has arrived at the place-based learning location, provide time for students to explore the area freely (under adult supervision). Provide access to materials such as digital cameras, magnifying glasses, tweezers, stretch gloves, and garden tools for exploration.

As students explore, pose questions for them to ponder. For example:

- What are you examining?
- Why is it interesting to you?
- What can you tell me about it?
- What do you wonder about it?

Encourage students to share their observations, thinking, and questions with teachers, peers, and other supervisors.

Regroup to discuss this initial exploration. Reflect on the predictions students made before the trip. Ask:

- What things did you think you would see on the trip? Smell? Hear? Feel?
- Were your predictions correct? Did you see, hear, smell, and feel what you thought you would?

- What surprised you?

Have students share their observations, ideas, and questions.

Explore Part Two

Provide students with empty pails. Explain to them that their job is to collect small, natural objects to take back to the classroom for further investigation. Ask:

- What kinds of things might we collect?

Brainstorm objects that can be used in Loose Parts bins (e.g., stones, leaves, twigs, shells, bark, seeds). Remind students to follow safety and environmental practices. This might include:

- wearing gloves when collecting
- only gathering objects from the ground (e.g., no pulling leaves off plants or twigs off trees, no picking flowers)
- considering what they could do to contribute to the environment from which they are taking something

Explore Part Three

Have students work in groups and choose one area or object of mutual interest to explore again. Have groups use string to create a border, so they can focus on one small area. Encourage students to share with each other their observations, ideas, and questions as they conduct deeper exploration.

Regroup to discuss this exploration. Have each group show the class their chosen area or object, and then share their observations, ideas, and questions. Guide the discussion with the Observe, Think, Wonder format:

- What did you observe in your area?
- What did you think about the area?
- What did you wonder about the area?

Encourage all students to share their observations, ideas, and questions. Focus on specific objects and materials as each group shares their chosen area or object. For example, ask:

- What kinds of objects do you see in this area? (e.g., rocks, leaves, sticks, grass, soil)
- Of what materials are the objects made? (e.g., stone, wood, plant material)
- Are there any objects in your area that are made by humans? (e.g., bench, sign, garbage bin, litter)
- Of what materials are these objects made? (e.g., plastic, wood, metal)

This is an excellent opportunity to discuss the impact of humans on the environment and to connect the First Peoples Principles of Learning related to the well-being of the land and recognizing the consequences of one's actions. Discuss environmentally friendly practices such as:

- leave only footprints (not litter)
- ensure plants are kept in their natural environment
- respect nests and other animal homes

Expand

To prepare students for journaling, do a journal entry together as a class. This will require a portable whiteboard and markers, or chart paper with a sturdy backboard.

As a class, choose a place to sit and journal. First, brainstorm journaling ideas together with students. For example, at the kindergarten to grade-two level, students may want to:

- sketch or colour objects in the natural environment
- sketch flowers or leaves
- identify emotions and record feelings about this natural environment (students may use happy faces, emojis, or their own designs for emojis)

▶

- make rubbings of natural items (e.g., leaves, bark, shells)
- photograph and sketch examples of matter in the natural environment
- draw and label diagrams
- draw a map of the local area or journaling location
- lie back to observe and sketch the sky
- use all senses to describe an object with pictures
- find a tree buddy, rock, or special place; sketch it, and give it a name

Work through a few journaling activities together. Then, distribute place-based journals and supplies to students (see page 61), and have them choose a place where they would like to sit and journal. Have students choose one journaling strategy to record. Use a digital camera to photograph students while they work on their journaling activity.

Formative Assessment

Photograph students as they journal to collect evidence of learning activities. Be sure to document students' thinking after journaling. Meet with students individually to have them share their thoughts about their observations of objects and materials in nature, the journaling experience, and what they recorded in their journal. Focus on their oral and written communication as they express and reflect on personal experiences of place. Use photographs taken as they journal to inspire reflection. Use the INDIVIDUAL STUDENT OBSERVATIONS template on page 51 to record interview highlights. Provide descriptive feedback to students about how they express and reflect on personal experiences of place.

Learning Centre A

At this learning centre, provide magnifying glasses, tweezers, paper plates, and the Loose Parts collection of objects gathered during the nature walk (e.g., seeds, nuts, twigs, leaves, rocks, shells). Place the objects in Loose Parts bins or pails (unsorted). Also, display photographs taken during the place-based learning activity and provide a copy of Learning-Centre Task Card A: How Can I Sort Objects From Nature? (2.1.1):

Download this template at <www.portageandmainpress.com/product/HOSMatterK2>.

Have students work in groups to examine the objects and describe their characteristics to peers, by making exploratory observations using their senses. Then have them sort the objects into the Loose Parts bins, based on their own sorting rules. Exploring these objects at the centre may also inspire further inquiry. Encourage students to ask questions and find ways to answer those questions, either at the centre or as personalized learning experiences.

1

Learning Centre B

At this learning centre, use the Loose Parts collections of sorted objects gathered on the nature walk (e.g., seeds, nuts, twigs, leaves, rocks, shells). Provide ledger-sized paper and crayons, along with a copy of Learning-Centre Task Card B: Counting Loose Parts (2.1.2):

Download this template at <www.portageandmainpress.com/product/HOSMatterK2>.

At the centre, have students take handfuls of objects, count them, and then display their work. Students may make simple charts for recording.

NOTE: Model the process of organizing and representing data. Conduct the learning-centre task first as a class, and have students suggest ways to show their work, such as the following:

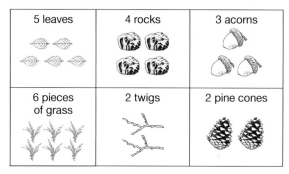

While this learning-centre task correlates with mathematics, it also provides an opportunity for students to focus on Curricular Competencies as they organize and present data.

Embed Part One: Talking Circle

NOTE: For more information about Talking Circles, see Talking Circles, page 16.

Revisit the guided inquiry question: **What do we observe, think, and wonder about objects and materials in nature?** Have students share their experiences and knowledge, provide examples, and ask further inquiry questions.

Embed Part Two

- Focus on students' use of the Core Competencies. Have students reflect on how they used one of the Core Competencies (Thinking, Communicating, or Personal and Social Skills) during the various lesson activities. Project one of the CORE COMPETENCY DISCUSSION PROMPTS templates (pages 38–42), and use it to inspire group reflection. Referring to the template, choose one or two "I Can" statements on which to focus. Students then use the "I Can" statements to provide evidence of how they demonstrated that competency. Ask

Properties of Matter for Grades K–2

questions directly related to that competency to inspire discussion. For example:

- Where did you get your ideas for your place-based journal entry today? (Creative Thinking)

Have students reflect orally, encouraging participation, questions, and the sharing of evidence (see page 29 for more information on these templates). As part of this process, students can also set goals. For example, ask:

- What would you do differently next time and why?
- How will you know if you are successful in meeting your goal?

■ To encourage self-reflection, provide prompts that students can use to cite examples of how they have used the Core Competencies in their learning. For this purpose, the CORE COMPETENCY SELF-REFLECTION FRAMES (pages 44–47) can be used throughout the learning process. There are five frames provided to address the Core Competencies: Communication, Creative Thinking, Critical Thinking, Positive Personal and Cultural Identity, and Personal Awareness and Responsibility. Conference individually with students to support self-reflection, or students may complete prompts using words and pictures. Again, have students set goals by considering what they might do differently on future tasks and how they will know if they are successful in meeting their goal.

NOTE: Use the same prompts from these templates over time to see how thinking changes with different activities.

Enhance

■ **Family Connection**: Provide students with the following sentence starter:

- When we go for a walk outdoors, we see objects and materials, such as _____.

Have students complete the sentence starter at home. Family members can help students draw and write about this topic. Have students share their sentences with the class.

■ Follow up this lesson's place-based learning activity with a class discussion about the experience. Construct an Observe, Think, Wonder chart as in the example below:

Observe	Think	Wonder

Have students share their ideas. Record these in the appropriate columns. Also have them compare observations to predictions discussed prior to the place-based learning experience.

2 | What Can We Learn About Objects and Materials Through Storytelling?

Information for Teachers

Storytelling makes learning more meaningful and engaging for students by connecting science concepts to real life and to other subjects. In this lesson, students will participate in a variety of storytelling experiences related to objects and materials.

This broad theme includes a wide range of fiction and nonfiction stories related to the use of objects and materials in everyday life, such as:

- building a house
- carving totem poles
- using camping equipment for certain weather conditions
- sewing, beading, knitting, or quilting
- cooking with utensils from a variety of cultures
- constructing a fly-fishing lure
- making a skating rink

Introduce students to new books with a book walk (see Engage). Use picture books related to objects and materials to provide students with opportunities to build background, enhance interest, generate questions, make predictions, examine visuals, learn new concepts, and share their growing knowledge with others.

Plan ahead to invite guest storytellers. Also encourage students to offer suggestions for storytellers from your local area, including family and community members.

If possible, invite a local Elder or Knowledge Keeper to participate in this learning experience. They may be able to share relevant stories about objects and materials.

NOTE: See Indigenous Perspectives and Knowledge, page 9, for guidelines for inviting Elders and Knowledge Keepers to speak to students.

Materials

- picture books about objects, materials, solids, liquids, and gases, including books by Indigenous authors and authors reflective of the community's cultural makeup (one book for each pair of students)
- *Duck and Goose* by Tad Hill (optional)
- Template: Sharing Stories Interview Guide (2.2.1)
- Learning-Centre Task Card: What Can I Learn About Objects and Materials? (2.2.2)
- drawing paper
- art supplies (e.g., pencil crayons, markers, pastels)

Engage

Model a book walk for students. Select a picture book about objects and materials, such as *Duck and Goose* by Tad Hill. In this story, Duck and Goose find an egg. They discuss how to care for the egg and all the things they will do with the "little occupant" when it comes out of the egg. They finally realize the egg is really a ball and go play with it. This is a great example of how the characteristics of an object can influence how an object is used.

Model the book walk with the following steps:

1. Show students the cover of the picture book.
2. Discuss the cover illustration.
3. Point out and discuss the various features of the cover, including the title, author, and illustrator.
4. Have students predict what the book is going to be about, based on their observations of the book's cover.
5. Walk through the pages, discussing the pictures but not reading the text. Ask questions about the illustrations. Have students share what they think is happening on each page.
6. Discuss the final illustrations, and have students predict how the story ends.

7. Discuss the sequence of events in the story.
8. Have students share how the book makes them feel, as well as what they wonder about the topic.
9. Have students share stories and experiences related to what they saw in the book.

After students have shared their ideas and experiences, read the book to the class.

Introduce the guided inquiry question: **What can we learn about objects and materials through storytelling?**

Explore Part One

Organize the class into pairs, and have each pair choose one picture book about objects and materials. Have pairs complete a book walk.

When they have completed the book walk, have each pair introduce their book to the class, presenting the pictures and their ideas about the content of the book.

In the days to follow, read each book aloud to the class. Focus on the objects and materials depicted in the books.

Explore Part Two

Many cultures exchange knowledge and history through oral storytelling. Provide an opportunity for students to benefit from these traditions to learn about objects and materials.

Invite a local Elder or Knowledge Keeper to share stories with the class. Stories may be related to topics such as building homes, making tools and clothing, beadwork, or totem design and construction. The oral storytelling process allows students an opportunity to learn why specific materials are used in particular objects.

NOTE: See Indigenous Perspectives and Knowledge, page 9, for guidelines for inviting Elders and Knowledge Keepers to speak to students.

Also consider inviting storytellers from other cultures, reflective of your local community, to share their oral traditions with the class.

To follow up oral storytelling experiences, read books by Indigenous authors about objects and materials, as well as books reflective of the class and community. Include these books at the learning centre.

Explore Part Three

Have students interview family members and ask them to share stories about objects and materials. Make sure students know to clearly ask permission to share the story publicly. Review with students that one of the First Peoples Principles of Learning recognizes that some knowledge is sacred and only shared with permission and/or in certain situations (see First Peoples Principles of Learning, page 12).

Story topics might include:

- hobbies (e.g., candle making, scrapbooking, baking and decorating a cake)
- home renovations (e.g., tiling a bathroom)
- gardening tools
- sports equipment (e.g., how objects such as tennis rackets or badminton birdies are made)
- beadwork

Students may come up with their own interview questions or use the Template: Sharing Stories Interview Guide (2.2.1):

2

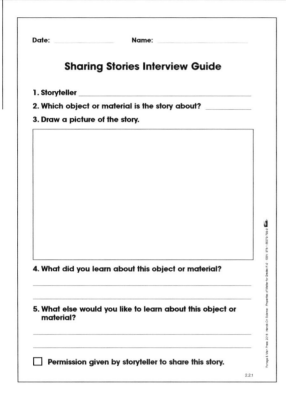

Download this template at <www.portageandmainpress.com/product/HOSMatterK2>.

NOTE: If using this template, review the activity before students take it home, so they are familiar with the questions. Family members may help complete the template. Students may also use other formats for recording these stories, including audio recordings, illustrations, or using traditional oral sharing techniques to retell the family story.

When students have completed this task at home, have them share their stories with the class. During their presentations, have students:

- tell the class about the person they interviewed
- provide a summary of the story
- explain how they know the story was about objects and materials

NOTE: Based on these interviews, students may be interested in inviting guests to share other stories about objects and materials. Family members, Elders and Knowledge Keepers, school staff, and community members who work with objects and materials may be invited to share stories and skills.

Expand

Have students explore storytelling about objects and materials further by posing their own inquiry questions for personalized learning. They may wish to:

- Initiate a project at the Makerspace centre, such as designing and constructing a structure to display a collection of books about objects and materials. (See page 19 and 62 for information about setting up a Makerspace centre.)
- Explore Loose Parts bins with various small objects made of one or more materials (e.g., wood, metal, plastic, paper). Students can explore the Loose Parts to generate their own inquiry questions.
- Make up their own oral stories about objects and materials to share with the class. This may be related to a hobby or interest (e.g., tell a story about building a fort, focusing on the building materials).
- Design and create models or puppets of characters from stories they have heard.
- Create a puppet theatre and recreate a story they have heard or made up themselves.
- Conduct an investigation or experiment based on their own inquiry questions.

As students explore and select ideas to expand learning, provide support and guidance as needed, and offer access to materials and resources that will enable students to conduct their chosen investigations.

Properties of Matter for Grades K–2

Learning Centre

NOTE: In preparation for this learning centre, model the activity together as a class to support students and make the activity more successful. Also explore and discuss questions such as:

- How do we read pictures?
- How do we find answers to our inquiry questions when we cannot read all the words in a book?

At the learning centre, set up an Objects and Materials Library with a variety of picture books about objects, materials, solids, liquids, and gases. Also, provide drawing paper, art supplies (e.g., pencil crayons, markers, pastels), and a copy of the Learning-Centre Task Card: What Can I Learn About Objects and Materials? (2.2.2):

Download this template at <www.portageandmainpress.com/product/HOSMatterK2>.

Have students choose anything they want to read from the library. Encourage them to do book walks, examine and discuss illustrations in the books, and share their ideas with peers. Students can then draw a picture reflective of their ideas.

NOTE: Depending on their literacy skills, students may choose to print the title and author of a book and create an illustration from the book.

Display students' work in the library for everyone to enjoy.

Embed Part One: Talking Circle

Revisit the guided inquiry question: **What can we learn about objects and materials through storytelling?** Have students share their experiences and knowledge, provide examples, and ask further inquiry questions.

Embed Part Two

- Focus on students' use of the Core Competencies. Have students reflect on how they used one of the Core Competencies (Thinking, Communicating, or Personal and Social Skills) during the various lesson activities. Project one of the CORE COMPETENCY DISCUSSION PROMPTS templates (pages 38–42), and use it to inspire group reflection. Referring to the template, choose one or two "I Can" statements on which to focus. Students then use the "I Can" statements to provide evidence of how they demonstrated that competency. Ask questions directly related to that competency to inspire discussion. For example:
  - How did you share your learning today? (Communication)

2

Have students reflect orally, encouraging participation, questions, and the sharing of evidence (see page 29 for more information on these templates).

As part of this process, students can also set goals. For example, ask:

- What would you do differently next time and why?
- How will you know if you are successful in meeting your goal?

- To encourage self-reflection, provide prompts that students can use to cite examples of how they have used the Core Competencies in their learning. For this purpose, the CORE COMPETENCY SELF-REFLECTION FRAMES (pages 44–47) can be used throughout the learning process. There are five frames provided to address the Core Competencies: Communication, Creative Thinking, Critical Thinking, Positive Personal and Cultural Identity, and Personal Awareness and Responsibility. Conference individually with students to support self-reflection, or students may complete prompts using words and pictures.

Again, have students set goals by considering what they might do differently on future tasks and how they will know if they are successful in meeting their goal.

NOTE: Use the same prompts from these templates over time to see how thinking changes with different activities.

3 | What Do We Know About Objects and Materials?

Materials

- digital cameras (one for each working group)
- printer (optional)
- computer/tablet with internet access (optional)
- magazines (optional)
- photo paper (optional)
- chart paper
- markers
- map of local area
- map of traditional territories of First Peoples in British Columbia (see lesson 1)
- sticky notes
- writing paper
- small plastic objects (e.g. buttons, beads, counters, cubes)
- small metal objects (e.g., coins, washers, paper clips)
- small wooden objects (e.g., beads, blocks, wood chips, sawdust)
- various small objects (e.g., rice, cotton balls, pom poms, shredded paper)
- audio-playing device with music
- empty paper-towel rolls
- wax paper
- elastic bands
- Learning-Centre Task Card: Shake It Up! (2.3.1)

SAFETY NOTE: Have students use caution when handling any material that might have sharp edges or splinters (e.g., scraps of metal, plastic, wood).

Engage Part One

NOTE: When conducting the following activity, consider having an adult supervisor help each working group.

Organize the class into four groups and provide a digital camera to each group. Assign each group one material—wood, plastic, metal, or paper. Explain to students that their mission is to find as many objects as they can that are made of their assigned material. Before beginning, demonstrate how to determine to which category an object belongs, as well as how to photograph the object. Encourage students to explore the classroom and the school for objects. Have students photograph objects they find. Ensure all students have an opportunity to photograph an object. Remind students they can photograph objects from the Loose Parts bins collected during the lesson 1 nature walk.

If possible, have students print their photos.

NOTE: Encourage students to also bring in or photograph items from home that fit into their group's material category.

Engage Part Two

Have each group present its collection of photographs to the class. Have groups discuss each item by naming it and identifying the material(s) of which the item is made.

NOTE: Some items will be made of only one material and can be identified as such, but other items will be made mostly of one material, with other secondary materials (e.g., metal scissors with plastic handles, wooden pencil with rubber eraser and metal fastener). Students should look for an item's primary material, but they may also identify an item's secondary materials.

When all groups have shared their photographs, introduce the guided inquiry question: **What do we know about objects and materials?**

Explore Part One

Continue the discussion from Engage Part Two as a class and, for each photograph, ask students to think about why the object they photographed is made of that material. For example, ask:

- Why do you think the door in the photograph is made of wood and not paper?

3

- Why do you think the faucet is made of metal and not fabric?
- What are the characteristics of each material?

On chart paper, create a herringbone chart, as in the following example:

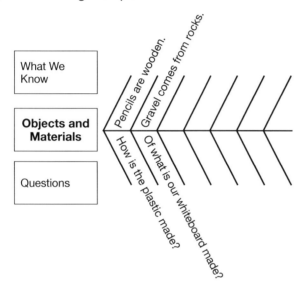

In the spaces above the horizontal line, record students' responses to "What We Know" about objects and materials.

Encourage students to reflect on the activities and discussions covered to this point in the module. Have them brainstorm a variety of questions (from basic knowledge to more complex analysis) about objects and materials to record in the lower section of the chart. For example:

- How is paper made?
- Why are some plastics strong and others not?
- What different materials are used to make my hockey skates?

Throughout the module, add more questions to the herringbone chart as students conduct various inquiries and pose new questions. Record answers to the questions below the corresponding question on the chart as students conduct investigations and research to build new knowledge.

Explore Part Two

Plan a nature walk around the neighbourhood to observe and collect natural objects. Consider inviting a local Elder or Knowledge Keeper to guide the nature walk to give students an opportunity to build their knowledge of how the characteristics of objects in nature make them useful resources in everyday life, both past and present.

NOTE: An Elder or Knowledge Keeper may want to tell stories associated with places around the school, or they may wish to talk about the resources found in the area. They might not talk about the characteristics of objects directly. See Indigenous Perspectives and Knowledge, page 9, for guidelines for inviting Elders and Knowledge Keepers to speak to students.

Before leaving the classroom, review the objects collected and photographed in Engage Part One. Ask:

- What kinds of objects did you collect?
- Of what materials are the different objects made?
- What kinds of objects could you collect from nature?

Before the walk, be sure to review with students the importance of respecting nature when collecting objects. Review the anchor chart created in lesson 1.

As with all place-based learning activities:

- Identify the importance of place. Use a map of the local area to identify where the location is in relation to the school.
- Identify on whose traditional territory the school is located, as well as the traditional territory of the location for the nature walk, if different.

▶

Properties of Matter for Grades K–2

- Incorporate land acknowledgment using local protocols.

(See lesson 1 for more information.)

NOTE: Review any other protocols for the walk. Give students an opportunity to ask questions and clarify expectations. Also, review safety issues (e.g., taking care when collecting objects that may have sharp edges).

Have students share with a classmate what they are most excited to see on this nature walk.

During the nature walk, stop to examine objects (e.g., trees, grasses, rocks). Have students use digital cameras to photograph these objects, and have students describe the object's characteristics. Discuss how various objects and materials are useful resources in everyday life. For example:

- trees are used to make lumber for building
- rocks are used to make driveways
- grass is used to feed livestock

Also discuss (or have the Elder/Knowledge Keeper discuss) how these natural materials are used by Indigenous peoples. For example:

- trees are used to make canoes and homes
- rocks are used to make tools
- grass Is woven to make mats

Small objects may also be collected to bring back to the classroom for use in subsequent lessons.

Explore Part Three

Have students search in magazines, online, or books in the classroom for pictures related to objects and materials. They may also use photographs taken on nature walks. Have each student choose one picture, identify all the materials in the picture, and label the materials using small sticky notes.

Display students' labelled pictures around the classroom, at the Objects and Materials Library, or on the word wall (see Explore Part Five).

Explore Part Four

With the class, discuss sustainability. In groups, have students examine the objects they photographed and discuss how the environment is affected by the use of that material. Model this process with an example (e.g., wood comes from trees, and forests are affected when humans cut down trees for lumber). Have students share their ideas, and record these on chart paper.

Also, introduce the terms *Reduce*, *Reuse*, and *Recycle* and write the terms on the chart paper. Students can further categorize items they photographed by identifying items that were made from recycled materials, speculating how they might reuse certain items, or trying to determine if they could reduce the usage of a certain object to preserve that material (e.g., paper towels). Record their ideas on chart paper.

Display this information in a place visible to students for the remainder of the module. Use the questions generated to guide future inquiry.

Explore Part Five

Begin a word wall to display new terms introduced throughout the module, as well as illustrations, photographs, and examples. When possible, add terminology in languages other than English, including Indigenous languages. This is a way of acknowledging and respecting students' cultural backgrounds, while enhancing learning for all students.

Words in English and languages other than English can be recorded in the first column, as in the following example:

Objects and Materials Word Wall	
Word	Pictures and Examples
rock (English) kéta (Northern Státimcets)	

NOTE: Online dictionaries may be used as a source for translations. For example:
- <www.firstvoices.com/en/Halqemeylem>

Online dictionaries are also available for other languages that may be reflective of the class cultural makeup.

As a class, discuss important words students have been using and learning about (e.g., wood). Record each term on the word wall and have students draw the term on a large sticky note. Depending on literacy levels, students can also label the parts of their drawing.

Expand

Provide students with an opportunity to further explore objects and materials by posing their own inquiry questions for personalized learning. They may wish to:

- Initiate a project at the Makerspace centre, such as designing and constructing a model object (e.g., castle, truck, desk) made of one or more materials.
- Explore Loose Parts bins with various small objects made of wood, metal, plastic, or paper, as well as objects made of more than one material. Students can explore the Loose Parts to generate their own inquiry questions.
- Create a piece of art using nature items from Loose Parts bins using an empty wooden picture frame (with the glass removed) with burlap covering the backing. Students can arrange objects and then photograph their creation for display. The objects can then be sorted and returned to the Loose Parts bins.
- Make and display a collection of objects made of one material.
- Build a structure made of one material (e.g., paper, wood, plastic).
- Construct a rock sculpture.
- Use recycled paper to make greeting cards.
- Conduct an investigation or experiment based on their own inquiry questions.

As students explore and select ideas to expand learning, provide support and guidance as needed, and offer access to materials and resources that will enable students to conduct their chosen investigations.

Learning Centre

At the learning centre, provide a variety of small objects of various materials in containers. For example:

- plastic (e.g., buttons, beads, counters, cubes)
- metal (e.g., coins, washers, paper clips)
- wood (e.g., beads, blocks, wood chips, sawdust)
- other (e.g., rice, cotton balls, pom poms, shredded paper)

Also provide empty paper-towel rolls, elastic bands, wax paper, an audio-playing device with music, and a copy of the Learning-Centre Task Card: Shake It Up! (2.3.1):

Learning Centre

Shake It Up!

Use the materials at the learning centre to make a shaker.

1. Cut a piece of wax paper to fit over one end of a cardboard roll.
2. Hold the wax paper in place with an elastic band.
3. Examine the objects in the different containers.
   - How are they the same?
   - How are they different?
4. Take a handful of objects from one container and place them in your cardboard roll.
5. Cover the open end of the roll with another piece of wax paper and another elastic band.
6. Your shaker is ready to try! Play the music and try out your shaker.
   - Can you play your shaker to the beat of the music?
7. Empty your shaker into the correct container, and make another shaker using objects in a different container.
   - How are the sounds from different objects the same?
   - How are they different?
   - Which is your favourite shaker sound?

2.3.1

Properties of Matter for Grades K–2

Download this template at <www.portageandmainpress.com/product/HOSMatterK2>.

Have students make shakers and compare the sounds made with different types of objects and materials.

Play music for students to accompany using their shakers.

Embed Part One: Talking Circle

Revisit the guided inquiry question: **What do we know about objects and materials?** Have students share their knowledge and experiences, provide examples, and ask further inquiry questions.

Embed Part Two

- Add to the herringbone chart as students learn new concepts, answer some of their own inquiry questions, and ask new inquiry questions.
- Add new terms and illustrations to the word wall. Include the words in languages other than English, such as Indigenous languages, as appropriate.
- Focus on students' use of the Core Competencies. Have students reflect on how they used one of the Core Competencies (Thinking, Communicating, or Personal and Social Skills) during the various lesson activities. Project one of the CORE COMPETENCY DISCUSSION PROMPTS templates (pages 38–42), and use it to inspire group reflection. Referring to the template, choose one or two "I Can" statements on which to focus. Students then use the "I Can" statements to provide evidence of how they demonstrated that competency. Ask questions directly related to that competency to inspire discussion. For example:
    - How did you decide which questions to ask today? (Critical Thinking)

  Have students reflect orally, encouraging participation, questions, and the sharing of evidence (see page 29 for more information on these templates).

  As part of this process, students can also set goals. For example, ask:
    - What would you do differently next time and why?
    - How will you know if you are successful in meeting your goal?

- To encourage self-reflection, provide prompts that students can use to cite examples of how they have used the Core Competencies in their learning. For this purpose, the CORE COMPETENCY SELF-REFLECTION FRAMES (pages 44–47) can be used throughout the learning process. There are five frames provided to address the Core Competencies: Communication, Creative Thinking, Critical Thinking, Positive Personal and Cultural Identity, and Personal Awareness and Responsibility. Conference individually with students to support self-reflection, or students may complete prompts using words and pictures.

Again, have students set goals by considering what they might do differently on future tasks and how they will know if they are successful in meeting their goal.

NOTE: Use the same prompts from these templates over time to see how thinking changes with different activities.

Enhance

- **Family Connection**: Provide students with the following sentence starter:
    - Some objects in our home made of different materials are _____.

3

Have students complete the sentence starter at home. Family members can help the student draw and write about objects and materials. Have students share their sentences with the class.

- Have students use an app (e.g., Pic Collage) to sort objects and create a collage of their photos taken by groups in Engage Part One.
- Provide several containers of small objects (e.g., yo-yos, balls, pencils, erasers, packs of chewing gum, acorns, stones), along with paper plates and index cards. Encourage students to sort the objects on paper plates according to their own rules and write the rules on the index cards.

To further extend this activity, have additional index cards with various sorting rules already printed on them, especially rules that students do not regularly use (e.g., pointed/not pointed, curved/straight edge). Have students use these rules to sort the objects onto the paper plates. Put picture clues on these index cards, so students do not have to rely on reading alone.

Encourage students to record their data using charts or pictographs. First model recording the data with the class, and then students can explore different graphic organizers for representing data. For example:

Sorting Rule	Number of Objects
pointed	5
no points	3
curves	0
straight edge	9

Properties of Matter for Grades K–2

4 How Can We Describe Objects and Materials?

Information for Teachers

It is important for students to use appropriate language to describe their observations of objects and materials. Encourage them to use qualitative observations to determine descriptive terms and phrases (e.g., *rough, smooth, shiny, dull, spongy, hollow sounding, echoes when tapped*). Also, encourage quantitative observations to describe relative size, thickness, mass, and length of objects.

Include descriptive terms and phrases on the word wall.

Materials

- chart paper*
- markers*
- plastic cups*
- paper cups*
- Styrofoam cups*
- plastic spoons*
- metal spoons*
- wooden spoons*
- objects and materials to examine and describe (e.g., classroom supplies, small toys, clothing items)
- large coffee can
- large socks
- small objects made of different materials (e.g., pencil, tennis ball, toy car, eraser, spoon, stick, pine cone, acorn, rock)
- paper bag
- glue
- scissors
- Learning-Centre Task Card: How Can I Describe Materials? (2.4.1)
- herringbone chart (from lesson 3)

*NOTE: Each working group will need one of each item marked with an asterisk.

Engage

Review the activities from lesson 3 with students. Ask:

- Which objects did you photograph?
- Of what materials were they made?

Ask for a volunteer.

Tell students they are to describe the volunteer. Remind students to use polite and kind words. Students may start with descriptors such as:

- hair colour (e.g., She has brown hair.)
- hair length, style, or texture (e.g., She has long hair; she has curly hair.)
- clothing (e.g., She is wearing a green shirt.)
- height (e.g., She is tall.)

Discuss with students that when they describe this person, they are describing their *characteristics*, which are features of something or someone that can be described using one (or more) of the senses. As a class, practise describing the characteristics of several more volunteers.

Then select several objects in the classroom (e.g., plant, chair, carpet). Have students describe the characteristics of these familiar objects. Encourage students to use as many of their senses as possible (and as appropriate) to determine how something looks, sounds, or feels (or, sometimes, how it smells). Encourage students to be very specific when making qualitative observations (e.g., a blue sweater could be better described as a soft and fuzzy navy-blue sweater).

Introduce the guided inquiry question: **How can we describe objects and materials?**

Explore Part One

Organize the class into working groups. Provide each group with chart paper, markers, and the following materials to examine: plastic cup, paper cup, Styrofoam cup, plastic spoon, metal spoon, and wooden spoon.

Give groups time to observe and discuss each object and brainstorm a list of words to describe that object. Ask students to record their ideas on chart paper, using words and pictures.

When all objects have been examined and described, have each group select one item to present to the rest of the class, sharing their descriptive words. Ensure each object is presented by at least one group.

When each object has been presented, ask:

- How are all these objects the same?
- How are they different?
- Of what kind(s) of material(s) is each object made?

During the discussion, encourage students to use detailed and accurate descriptors for the objects (e.g., the metal spoon is smooth and shiny). Also, model for students how to describe objects according to quantitative characteristics (e.g., a wooden spoon is longer than a drinking straw, a plastic cup is bigger than a hand).

Student Self-Assessment

Have students complete the COOPERATIVE SKILLS SELF-ASSESSMENT template, on page 49, to reflect on their success working with others as they shared and compared ideas.

Formative Assessment

Observe students as they conduct the group inquiry with the various objects. Complete the COOPERATIVE SKILLS TEACHER ASSESSMENT template, on page 52, to reflect on students' ability to work with others as they share and compare ideas. Provide descriptive feedback to students about how they collaborate with others.

Explore Part Two

Have each student select one of the objects used in the previous activities or a new object of their choice from the classroom. Explain to students that their task is to create a riddle about their object. They are to think of three clues that describe three characteristics of their object. Stress that one of the characteristic clues should include the material of which the object is made. For example:

- My object is smooth.
- My object is made of metal.
- My object feels cold.
- What object is it?

Use the Optimal Learning Model (I do, We do, You do; see pages 26–27 for more information). Begin by selecting an object and creating a riddle for students. Then, select an object and create a riddle together. Finally, have students create their own riddles. Students may record their riddles on paper or share them orally.

When all students have completed their riddles, display the objects. Have students share their riddles orally or read them for the class, then work as a class to match the riddle with the object it describes.

Expand

Provide students with an opportunity to explore the characteristics of objects and materials further by posing their own inquiry questions for personalized learning. They may wish to:

- Initiate a project at the Makerspace centre, such as designing and constructing a case to display specific objects (e.g., baseball cards) or objects made of a specific material (e.g., a rock collection).
- Explore Loose Parts bins with various small objects with varying characteristics, including texture (e.g., rough, smooth, soft, hard),

▶

Properties of Matter for Grades K–2

shape (e.g., round, flat, edges), colour, and size. Students can explore the Loose Parts to generate their own inquiry questions.
- Write and illustrate a riddle book about various objects and materials.
- Use a list of characteristics to create a text-visual using an online tool (e.g., Wordle) as in the following example:

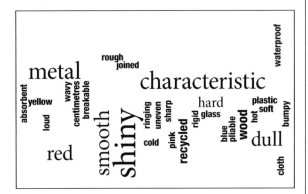

- Conduct an investigation or experiment based on their own inquiry questions. Consider reminding students of questions posed earlier in the module (e.g., from their nature walks).

As students explore and select ideas to expand learning, provide support and guidance as needed, and offer access to materials and resources that will enable students to conduct their chosen investigations.

Learning Centre

At the learning centre, provide a variety of small objects made of different materials (e.g., pencil, tennis ball, toy car, eraser, spoon, stick, pine cone, acorn, rock). Place the objects in a paper bag, with the top folded. Make a mystery can by gluing an old sock over a large coffee can. Cut a hole in the end of the sock, large enough for a student's hand. Also provide a copy of the Learning-Centre Task Card: How Can I Describe Materials? (2.4.1):

Download this template at <www.portageandmainpress.com/product/HOSMatterK2>.

Have students work in pairs. Have one student select an item from the bag, without looking in the bag or letting their partner see the object. Have them place the object into the mystery can. Their partner will then put their hand in the mystery can, describe the object, and try to identify it. Have partners change roles and play until all objects have been guessed.

Embed Part One: Talking Circle

Revisit the guided inquiry question: **How can we describe objects and materials?** Have students share their knowledge and experiences, provide examples, and ask further inquiry questions.

90 Hands-On Science: An Inquiry Approach • Grades K–2

4

Embed Part Two

- Add to the herringbone chart as students learn new concepts, answer some of their own inquiry questions, and ask new inquiry questions.

- Add new terms and illustrations to the word wall. Include the words in languages other than English, such as Indigenous languages, as appropriate.

- Focus on students' use of the Core Competencies. Have students reflect on how they used one of the Core Competencies (Thinking, Communicating, or Personal and Social Skills) during the various lesson activities. Project one of the CORE COMPETENCY DISCUSSION PROMPTS templates (pages 38–42), and use it to inspire group reflection. Referring to the template, choose one or two "I Can" statements on which to focus. Students then use the "I Can" statements to provide evidence of how they demonstrated that competency. Ask questions directly related to that competency to inspire discussion. For example:
  - How did you grow as a learner today? (Positive Personal and Cultural Identity)

  Have students reflect orally, encouraging participation, questions, and the sharing of evidence (see page 29 for more information on these templates).

  As part of this process, students can also set goals. For example, ask:
  - What would you do differently next time and why?
  - How will you know if you are successful in meeting your goal?

- To encourage self-reflection, provide prompts that students can use to cite examples of how they have used the Core Competencies in their learning. For this purpose, the CORE COMPETENCY SELF-REFLECTION FRAMES (pages 44–47) can be used throughout the learning process. There are five frames provided to address the Core Competencies: Communication, Creative Thinking, Critical Thinking, Positive Personal and Cultural Identity, and Personal Awareness and Responsibility. Conference individually with students to support self-reflection, or students may complete prompts using words and pictures.

Again, have students set goals by considering what they might do differently on future tasks and how they will know if they are successful in meeting their goal.

NOTE: Use the same prompts from these templates over time to see how thinking changes with different activities.

Enhance

- **Family Connection**: Provide students with the following sentence starter:
  - We can describe different objects in our home, such as _____.

  Have students complete the sentence starter at home. Family members can help the student draw and write about this topic. Have students share their sentences with the class.

- Access the interactive activity, Sorting Soft, Smooth, and Scratchy Stuff, from the Unit 2 folder in the ***Hands-On Science and Technology, Grade 1*** download. While these interactive activities were originally developed for the Ontario curriculum, they present valuable learning opportunities across grades and provincial curriculums. Find this download at: <https://www.portageandmainpress.com/product/hands-on-interactive-for-science-and-technology-grade-1>.

5 | How Can We Sort Objects and Materials?

Materials

- household and classroom objects made of different materials (e.g., wood, metal, plastic, rubber, paper, cloth)
- Hula-Hoops
- index cards
- markers
- scissors
- glue
- magazines, flyers, and catalogues
- small wooden objects (e.g., toothpicks, bark, wood shavings)
- small plastic objects (e.g., cutlery, plastic wrap, bread clips, bingo chips)
- small metal objects (e.g., paper clips, staples, aluminum foil, nails, screws, bolts)
- cloth samples (e.g., yarn, wool, thread, various swatches of fabric)
- paper objects (e.g., plates, napkins, wrapping paper, stickers)
- poster paper
- ledger-size paper
- Learning-Centre Task Card: Make a Materials Collage! (2.5.1)
- herringbone chart (from lesson 3)

Engage

Review the term *characteristic* and refer to the word wall. Have students work in pairs to describe three characteristics of each other (e.g., brown hair, green eyes, freckles). When students are finished, ask a few pairs to share their characteristics.

Gather students into a circle. Place the household and classroom objects in the middle of the circle. Pass the items around the circle, so each student has a chance to examine and describe each item.

Have students sort the household and classroom objects according to the material from which each is made, then place the objects inside the Hula-Hoops according to material. Label each Hula-Hoop with an index card. Students will notice that some objects are made of more than one material. Leave these objects out of the sorted groups, add additional groups, or, depending on student's prior knowledge, introduce Venn diagrams. For example:

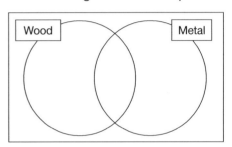

Introduce the guided inquiry question: **How can we sort objects and materials?**

Explore

Provide each student with a variety of magazines, flyers, and catalogues, as well as scissors, glue, and ledger-size paper. Have students find and cut out pictures of items that are made of wood, cloth, metal, glass, paper, and plastic. Then, ask students to sort their pictures by material and glue the pictures onto the paper in labelled circles, as in the following example:

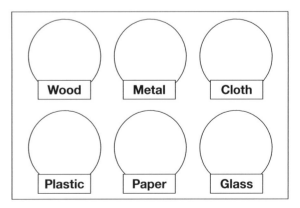

Formative Assessment (PA)

Observe students as they describe and classify materials, build their sorting mats and/or Venn diagrams with Hula-Hoops, and create their collages. Encourage them to ask and answer their own questions about sorting objects and materials. Use the ANECDOTAL RECORD template, on page 50, to record results. Provide descriptive feedback to students about how they describe and classify materials.

Expand

Provide students with an opportunity to explore sorting objects and materials further by posing their own inquiry questions for personalized learning. They may wish to:

- Initiate a project at the Makerspace centre, such as designing and constructing a structure made of a specific number and kind of materials (e.g., wood and metal, plastic and paper).
- Explore Loose Parts bins with various small objects made of wood, metal, plastic, and paper, as well as objects made of more than one material. Students can explore the Loose Parts to generate their own inquiry questions.
- Sort collections other than by the materials from which they are made, and then design a graphic organizer to present their sorting.
- Conduct tests on a variety of same-material objects found in the classroom. For example:
  - Test pieces of wood for softness by scratching them with a nail or by hitting them with a hammer.
  - Rate metals for shininess by ordering them from shiniest to dullest.
  - Test rock samples for hardness with a nail scratch test.
  - Compare the thickness of various types of cloth.
  - Compare fabric samples for smoothness.
- Conduct an investigation or experiment based on their own inquiry questions.

As students explore and select ideas to expand learning, provide support and guidance as needed, and offer access to materials and resources that will enable students to conduct their chosen investigations.

Learning Centre

At the learning centre, provide poster paper, scissors, glue, and a variety of objects made of different materials such as:

- wood (e.g., toothpicks, bark, wood shavings)
- plastic (e.g., cutlery, plastic wrap, bread clips, bingo chips)
- metal (e.g., paper clips, staples, aluminum foil, nails, screws, bolts)
- cloth (e.g., yarn, wool, thread, various fabrics)
- paper (e.g., plates, napkins, wrapping paper, stickers)

Also, provide a copy of the Learning-Centre Task Card: Make a Materials Collage! (2.5.1):

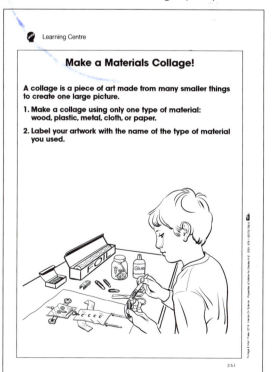

Properties of Matter for Grades K–2

Download this template at <www.portageandmainpress.com/product/HOSMatterK2>.

Have students create collages made of only one type of material. Have them title their picture with the name of the material used (e.g., Metal).

Embed Part One: Talking Circle

Revisit the guided inquiry question: **How can we sort objects and materials?** Have students share their experiences and knowledge, provide examples, and ask further inquiry questions.

Embed Part Two

- Add to the herringbone chart as students learn new concepts, answer some of their own inquiry questions, and ask new inquiry questions.
- Add new terms and illustrations to the word wall. Include the words in languages other than English, such as Indigenous languages, as appropriate.
- Focus on students' use of the Core Competencies. Have students reflect on how they used one of the Core Competencies (Thinking, Communicating, or Personal and Social Skills) during the various lesson activities. Project one of the CORE COMPETENCY DISCUSSION PROMPTS templates (pages 38–42), and use it to inspire group reflection. Referring to the template, choose one or two "I Can" statements on which to focus. Students then use the "I Can" statements to provide evidence of how they demonstrated that competency. Ask questions directly related to that competency to inspire discussion. For example:
  - What are you proud of in your learning today? (Personal Awareness and Responsibility)

Have students reflect orally, encouraging participation, questions, and the sharing of evidence (see page 29 for more information on these templates).

As part of this process, students can also do some goal setting. Ask:
- What would you do differently next time and why?
- How will you know if you are successful in meeting your goal?

- To further encourage self-reflection, provide prompts that students can use to cite examples of how they have used the Core Competencies in their learning. For this purpose, the CORE COMPETENCY SELF-REFLECTION FRAMES on pages 43–47 can be used throughout the learning process. There are five frames provided to address the Core Competencies, one each on Communication, Creative Thinking, Critical Thinking, Positive Personal and Cultural Identity, and Personal Awareness and Responsibility. Conference individually with students to support self-reflection, or students may complete prompts using words and pictures. Again, involve students in goal setting by having them consider what they might do differently on future tasks, and how they will know if they are successful in meeting their goal.

NOTE: Use the same prompts from these templates over time to see how thinking changes with different activities.

Enhance

- **Family Connection**: Provide students with the following sentence starter:
  - We can sort different objects in our home, such as _____.

Have students complete the sentence starter at home. Family members can help the student draw and write about this topic. Have students share their sentences with the class.

- Have each student complete the Explore Part One activity at home, using drawings or photographs of objects found around the home and sorted according to the materials from which the objects are made.

- Access the interactive activity, Sorting by Material, from the Unit 2 folder in the *Hands-On Science and Technology, Grade 1* download. While these interactive activities were originally developed for the Ontario curriculum, they present valuable learning opportunities across grades and provincial curriculums. Find this download at: <https://www.portageandmainpress.com/product/hands-on-interactive-for-science-and-technology-grade-1/>.

6 | Why Are Some Materials Better Than Others for Certain Jobs?

Materials

- four bowls, labelled A, B, C, and D
- apple (whole)
- potato (whole)
- timer
- paring knife*
- plastic knife*
- butter knife*
- vegetable peeler*
- potato masher*
- cutting board
- index cards
- plastic food wrap
- Template: Why Are Some Materials Better Than Others for Certain Jobs? (2.6.1)
- chart paper
- markers
- Image Bank: Tools of First Peoples in British Columbia (see Appendix, page 175)
- projection device (optional)
- computer/tablet with internet access (optional)
- Learning-Centre Task Card: What If…? (2.6.2)
- herringbone chart (from lesson 3)

 ***SAFETY NOTE:** Kitchen utensils are for teacher use only.

Engage

Have students observe and examine the apple and the potato. Ask them to describe the inside and outside of each.

NOTE: Students can use background knowledge to describe the inside of the potato and the apple.

Record their descriptions on chart paper.

Have students compare and contrast the outside and the inside of the apple and the potato.

Ask:

- How are the outside of the apple and the outside of the potato the same?
- How are they different?
- How are the inside of the apple and the inside of the potato the same?
- How are they different?

Next, focus on tools used to peel, cut, and mash the potato and the apple. Do not display the utensils at this point. Ask:

- What might I use to cut up the potato and the apple?
- What might I use to peel each?
- What if I wanted to make mashed potatoes or apple sauce? How could I mash them?

As each question is asked, have students discuss their background knowledge of these utensils (e.g., knife, peeler, masher). Discuss the design of each and how it is used. Have students role-play peeling, cutting, and mashing the potato or the apple.

Introduce the guided inquiry question: **Why are some materials better than others for certain jobs?**

Explore Part One

 SAFETY NOTE: During this activity, teachers will be cutting the potato and the apple. Review safety rules before using knives, and stress that students should not use sharp utensils.

Now display—but do not identify—the paring knife, plastic knife, butter knife, vegetable peeler, and potato masher. Have students describe each knife and the peeler, and predict which utensil is best for removing the skin from the apple and the potato. Record their predictions on chart paper. Test their predictions by trying to peel the apple and the potato with each knife and the peeler.

6

Ask:

- Which utensil works best? Why?

Finish peeling the apple and the potato.

Now, ask students to predict which utensil is best for slicing the apple and the potato. Record their predictions on chart paper. Test their predictions by trying to slice the apple and the potato with each of the knives and with the peeler. Ask:

- Which utensil works best? Why?

Finish slicing the apple and the potato.

Have students observe and examine the slices. Ask:

- What do you think will happen if we leave these slices on the table for a long time?
- Why do you think this will happen?
- Why do you think the apple and the potato will turn brown?
- Can you think of a way we could stop the apple and the potato from turning brown?
- What could we use?

Place half of the apple slices in bowl A, uncovered. Wrap the other apple slices in plastic wrap, and place them in bowl B. Do the same with the potato slices, and place in bowls C and D.

Use the Template: Why Are Some Materials Better Than Others for Certain Jobs? (2.6.1) or recreate the chart on chart paper:

Download this template at <www.portageandmainpress.com/product/HOSMatterK2>.

Point to the word *prediction*, and review with students that a *prediction* is a guess about what will happen.

Have students predict what will happen to the apple slices and the potato slices if they are left in the bowls for 20 minutes, 40 minutes, and one hour. Record their predictions on the chart. Students may volunteer to add illustrations to the chart as well, to reflect their predictions.

NOTE: Although students at the kindergarten to grade-two level are not required to measure the passage of time in standard units, they might think of 20 minutes as the same (or almost the same) amount of time as recess or a particular TV show. Have a discussion with students about the passage of time, and how to use a timer (as opposed to a clock) to measure passage of time for this activity. Visual timers are available online, such as <https://www.online-stopwatch.com/countdown-clock/>.

Properties of Matter for Grades K–2

6

Continue with other classroom activities. Every 20 minutes, have students examine the apples and the potatoes again. Point to the word *observation* at the top of the second column of the chart, and explain that *observation* means what really happens in an experiment. Record students' observations on the chart. Have students infer why the apples and the potatoes wrapped in plastic wrap did not go brown. Discuss the characteristics of the plastic wrap that make it useful for preventing the apple slices and the potato slices from turning brown quickly. Also, discuss other ways plastic wrap is used (e.g., wrap sandwiches and other foods for lunch, wrap leftovers from dinner).

NOTE: Students do not need to provide a complex scientific explanation. They can simply say that when the apple and potato slices are covered with plastic wrap, the slices will not turn brown quickly because the air cannot touch them. A characteristic of plastic wrap is that it does not let air through.

Student Self-Assessment

Have students use the SCIENCE JOURNAL template, on page 37, to reflect on what they learned during this lesson's investigation. Students can draw pictures to record observations. Teachers or other classroom helpers may also scribe to complete the template.

Explore Part Two

Introduce students to tools of Indigenous peoples in British Columbia. Invite a local Elder or Knowledge Keeper to share and demonstrate the use of tools.

NOTE: See Indigenous Perspectives and Knowledge, page 9, for guidelines for inviting Elders and Knowledge Keepers to speak to students.

Display the Image Bank: Tools of First Peoples in British Columbia, which depicts tools used by different Indigenous peoples. As each image is projected, have students:

- describe the characteristics of the tool
- predict how the tool is made and what materials are used
- predict the tool's use

As students share their ideas, provide background information (included in the Appendix, on page 175). Discuss why certain materials are used in the construction of these tools. It is important for students to understand how tools are related to place. Different tools are needed in different locations. Different materials are available in different locations. No one tool is used by all Indigenous peoples, as tools are specific to location, traditions, and need.

NOTE: Consider taking a field trip to a local museum or Indigenous community that may have collections of similar artifacts from Indigenous peoples specific to your area. Also consider guided visits to local totem poles to learn about the tools used to carve and raise the totem.

Expand

Provide students with an opportunity to explore objects and materials further by posing their own inquiry questions for personalized learning. They may wish to:

- Initiate a project at the Makerspace centre, such as designing and constructing a lunch bag or thermal bag.
- Explore Loose Parts related to materials used for specific jobs. Collect various small kitchen objects and tools (e.g., cutlery, bread clips, twist ties, plastic wrap, aluminum foil, wax paper, parchment paper). Students can explore the Loose Parts to generate their own inquiry questions.
- Conduct investigations to find out what other materials would stop the apple slices and the potato slices from turning brown (e.g., plastic bags, paper bags, aluminum foil, wax paper).

6

- Explore tools and devices related to special interests (e.g., skiing, skating, fishing, dance) to determine which materials are used and what purpose they serve.
- Conduct an investigation or experiment based on their own inquiry questions.

As students explore and select ideas to expand learning, provide support and guidance as needed, and offer access to materials and resources that will enable students to conduct their chosen investigations.

Learning Centre

At the learning centre, provide index cards, markers, and a copy of the Learning-Centre Task Card: What If…? (2.6.2):

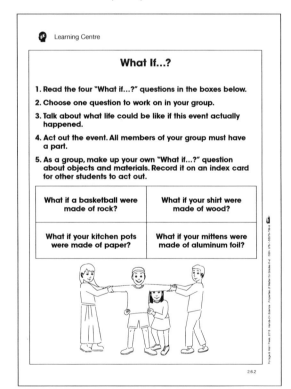

Download this template at <www.portageandmainpress.com/product/HOSMatterK2>.

Have students play "What If…?," with a focus on properties of materials. Ask students to imagine what would happen in the following situations:

- What if a basketball were made of rock?
- What if your shirt were made of wood?
- What if your kitchen pots were made of paper?
- What if your mittens were made of aluminum foil?

Have students work together to answer the questions. Have them discuss the material that each item is really made from and the properties of those materials (e.g., a basketball is made of rubber, because rubber bounces). Students also have the opportunity to create their own "What if…?" question and record it on an index card.

Have pairs of students act out the "What If…?" situations for their classmates.

Embed Part One: Talking Circle

Revisit the guided inquiry question: **Why are some materials better than others for certain jobs?** Have students share their knowledge and experiences, provide examples, and ask further inquiry questions.

Embed Part Two

- Add to the herringbone chart as students learn new concepts, answer some of their own inquiry questions, and ask new inquiry questions.
- Add new terms and illustrations to the word wall. Include the words in languages other than English, such as Indigenous languages, as appropriate.
- Focus on students' use of the Core Competencies. Have students reflect on how they used one of the Core Competencies (Thinking, Communicating, or Personal and Social Skills) during the various lesson activities. Project one of

▶

the CORE COMPETENCY DISCUSSION PROMPTS templates (pages 38–42), and use it to inspire group reflection. Referring to the template, choose one or two "I Can" statements on which to focus. Students then use the "I Can" statements to provide evidence of how they demonstrated that competency. Ask questions directly related to that competency to inspire discussion. For example:

- How did you make safe choices today? (Personal Awareness and Responsibility)

Have students reflect orally, encouraging participation, questions, and the sharing of evidence (see page 29 for more information on these templates).

As part of this process, students can also set goals. For example, ask:

- What would you do differently next time and why?
- How will you know if you are successful in meeting your goal?

- To encourage self-reflection, provide prompts that students can use to cite examples of how they have used the Core Competencies in their learning. For this purpose, the CORE COMPETENCY SELF-REFLECTION FRAMES (pages 44–47) can be used throughout the learning process. There are five frames provided to address the Core Competencies: Communication, Creative Thinking, Critical Thinking, Positive Personal and Cultural Identity, and Personal Awareness and Responsibility. Conference individually with students to support self-reflection, or students may complete prompts using words and pictures.

Again, have students set goals by considering what they might do differently on future tasks, and how they will know if they are successful in meeting their goal.

NOTE: Use the same prompts from these templates over time to see how thinking changes with different activities.

Enhance

- **Family Connection**: Provide students with one or both of the following sentence starters:
  - Some tools we use at home are _____.
  - Some tools my family members use for their jobs are _____.

  Have students complete the sentence starter at home. Family members can help the student draw and write about this topic. Have students share their sentences with the class.

- Explore the use of other kitchen utensils (e.g., lifters, wooden spoons, spatulas). Discuss the materials from which different objects are made, and how that material makes the utensil useful.

- As an extension to the learning-centre activity, have students come up with their own "What if…?" question. Have them illustrate the question, and create a class book or display on a bulletin board. Do a shared write on the first page of the book, in which the class explains to others what they are learning.

- Go on a field trip to a local bakery (or other business) to investigate the tools and devices used on the job.

- Invite guest speakers, including family members, who use specific tools for their job or hobby (e.g., carpenter, electrician, mechanic, nurse).

- Encourage students to think of how they could be more environmentally conscious about their own use of materials (e.g., reuse zipper-lock storage bags or aluminum foil, use plastic food containers). Students may also suggest the use of lemon juice to

▶

6

prevent food from turning brown. Ask which methods are more sustainable.

- To focus on creativity, have students come up with alternative uses for everyday objects. See the following link for examples: <www.indiana.edu/~bobweb/Handout/d1.uses.htm>.

> **SAFETY NOTE:** The following activity has students observing carpentry tools. Preface the activity by promoting safety awareness when handling tools that can cause injury if caution is not used at all times. Have additional adults to supervise this activity.

- Have students examine and manipulate carpentry tools (e.g., hammer, screwdriver, sandpaper, nail, tape measure, pliers). Focus on the function of each tool and the material(s) of which it is made. Discuss that both the material(s) the tool is made of and how the tool is constructed affect the function of the tool. Some materials can be more easily changed (e.g., manipulated—cut, sanded, chiseled) by a smooth edge, others by a serrated edge, each of which performs a different function.

- Access the interactive activity, Matching Materials With Tools, from the Unit 2 folder in the *Hands-On Science and Technology, Grade 1* download. While these interactive activities were originally developed for the Ontario curriculum, they present valuable learning opportunities across grades and provincial curriculums. Find this download at: <https://www.portageandmainpress.com/product/hands-on-interactive-for-science-and-technology-grade-1/>.

Properties of Matter for Grades K–2

7 How Can Different Materials Be Used to Construct Objects?

Materials

- various versions of *Goldilocks and the Three Bears*
- upholstered chair
- metal chair
- wooden chair
- drawing paper
- variety of bear stuffies (of a suitable size for students to build beds, or have students bring a favourite stuffie, providing it meets size requirements)
- materials for building beds for bears (e.g., shoeboxes, cereal and cracker boxes, fabric scraps, pillow stuffing, small pillows, small blankets/towels/cloths, packing tape, paper-towel rolls)*
- projection device (optional)
- Image Bank: Canoes (see Appendix, page 175)
- wood and bark samples from cedar (red and yellow), cottonwood, and birch trees
- Learning-Centre Task Card: Build a Bed for Your Bear (2.7.1)
- herringbone chart (from lesson 3)

*NOTE: Send a letter home with students asking for assistance in collecting materials for building bear beds.

Engage

Read a version of *Goldilocks and the Three Bears* to students. Discuss the story, and focus on the chairs. Ask:

- What was wrong with Mother Bear's chair?
- What was wrong with Father Bear's chair?
- Why was Baby Bear's chair just right?
- Of what do you think the chairs in the story were made?

Discuss students' responses to these questions.

Introduce the guided inquiry question: **How can different materials be used to construct objects?**

Explore Part One

Present three chairs to students—a metal chair, a wooden chair, and an upholstered chair. Ask:

- For what are chairs used?
- How are all these chairs the same?
- How are they different?
- From what is each chair made?
- From where does wood come?
- Which is the strongest chair? Why?

Have students examine each chair. Have them focus on the materials used to make the chair, and how the chair is constructed. Provide each student with drawing paper. Have them draw a picture of each chair and, as appropriate to literacy levels, record how the chairs are similar to and different from each other.

Have students share their pictures and comparisons with a partner. Then, as a class, discuss how the chairs are similar to and different from each other.

Explore Part Two

Have students explore canoe construction. Indigenous peoples use canoes for many different purposes (e.g., racing, travelling by river or ocean, transporting goods). Canoes are usually made from materials available in the local area. Often large trees, such as red or yellow cedar, are hollowed out. In British Columbia's interior, cottonwood is often used to build canoes.

Invite a local Elder or Knowledge Keeper to share stories and information about canoes and the materials from which they are made. This guest may also discuss how Indigenous people use other local materials to make useful products (e.g., vines for rope, mountain goat horns for spoons).

NOTE: See Indigenous Perspectives and Knowledge, page 9, for guidelines for inviting Elders and Knowledge Keepers to speak to students.

Display the Image Bank: Canoes. Have students discuss the characteristics of the various boats, focusing on similarities, differences, materials (see descriptions in the Appendix), and designs. Have students examine and manipulate wood and bark samples from cedar (red and yellow), cottonwood, and birch trees. Discuss the characteristics of these materials and how they are useful in making canoes.

Expand

Provide students with an opportunity to explore how to build objects using different materials further by posing their own inquiry questions for personalized learning. They may wish to:

- Initiate a project at the Makerspace centre, such as designing and constructing a structure made solely of recycled newspaper.
- Explore Loose Parts related to constructing objects with various item for building (e.g., tools, fasteners, nails, screws, bolts). Students can explore the Loose Parts to generate their own inquiry questions.
- Explore objects made of different materials at home. For example, draw pictures of the different doors in their homes and identify the characteristics and materials used for each door.
- Explore objects made of different materials in the community. For example, draw pictures of the different playground structures and identify the characteristics and materials used for each.
- Conduct an investigation or experiment based on their own inquiry questions.

As students explore and select ideas to expand learning, provide support and guidance as needed, and offer access to materials and resources that will enable students to conduct their chosen investigations.

Learning Centre

At the learning centre, provide a variety of bear stuffies, various materials for making beds for the bears (e.g., shoeboxes, cereal and cracker boxes, fabric scraps, pillow stuffing, small pillows, small blankets/towels/cloths, packing tape, paper-towel rolls), along with a copy of the Learning-Centre Task Card: Build a Bed for Your Bear (2.7.1):

Download this template at <www.portageandmainpress.com/product/HOSMatterK2>.

7

Have students select a bear from the collection. Then, have students select whatever materials they need to build a suitable bed for their bear.

Ensure versions of *Goldilocks and the Three Bears* are available at the centre for students to reference.

Formative Assessment

Before having students work at the learning centre, co-create criteria for the bed's design and construction. For example:

- My animal fits in its bed.
- My bed is comfortable for my animal.
- My bed is made of at least three materials.
- The materials used in my bed are labelled.

Conference with students individually, and have them present their bed. Encourage them to make explanatory observations about how their bed meets the criteria. Also encourage students to identify materials used in the bed construction and how the features of those materials made for a good choice. Use the INDIVIDUAL STUDENT OBSERVATIONS template, on page 51, to record results. Provide descriptive feedback to students about how they make explanatory observations.

Embed Part One: Talking Circle

Revisit the guided inquiry question: **How can different materials be used to construct objects?** Have students share their knowledge and experiences, provide examples, and ask further inquiry questions.

Embed Part Two

- Add to the herringbone chart as students learn new concepts, answer some of their own inquiry questions, and ask new inquiry questions.
- Add new terms and illustrations to the word wall. Include the words in languages other than English, such as Indigenous languages, as appropriate.
- Focus on students' use of the Core Competencies. Have students reflect on how they used one of the Core Competencies (Thinking, Communicating, or Personal and Social Skills) during the various lesson activities. Project one of the CORE COMPETENCY DISCUSSION PROMPTS templates (pages 38–42), and use it to inspire group reflection. Referring to the template, choose one or two "I Can" statements on which to focus. Students then use the "I Can" statements to provide evidence of how they demonstrated that competency. Ask questions directly related to that competency to inspire discussion. For example:
  - How did you show that you were an active listener today? (Communication)

Have students reflect orally, encouraging participation, questions, and the sharing of evidence (see page 29 for more information on these templates).

As part of this process, students can also set goals. For example, ask:

- What would you do differently next time and why?
- How will you know if you are successful in meeting your goal?

- To encourage self-reflection, provide prompts that students can use to cite examples of how they have used the Core Competencies in their learning. For this purpose, the CORE COMPETENCY SELF-REFLECTION FRAMES (pages 44–47) can be used throughout the learning process. There are five frames provided to address the Core Competencies: Communication, Creative Thinking, Critical Thinking, Positive Personal and Cultural Identity, and Personal Awareness and Responsibility. Conference individually with students to support self-reflection, or students may complete prompts using words and pictures.

Again, have students set goals by considering what they might do differently on future tasks, and how they will know if they are successful in meeting their goal.

NOTE: Use the same prompts from these templates over time to see how thinking changes with different activities.

Enhance

- **Family Connection**: Provide students with one of the following sentence starters:
    - We are glad our home is constructed of _____ because _____.

    We are glad _____ (an item at home) is made of _____ because _____. Have students complete their sentence starter at home. Family members can help the student draw and write about this topic. Have students share their sentences with the class.

- Have students order the chairs from Explore Part One according to mass or comfort. Students could also predict the strength of each chair (and order them by strength) based on materials and construction.

- As a class, measure the height of the chairs from floor to seat or back using interlocking cubes, and then order them accordingly (from shortest to tallest seat or back). Height could also be measured using pieces of string, which could then be displayed on a graph.

- To explore the use of natural materials for specific purposes, have students conduct an inquiry into how various animals make their beds. For example:
    - What does a deer use for its bed?
    - How does a bird build its nest?
    - What bedding does a squirrel use?

- Collect bird and wasp nests (or photographs) for students to examine. Discuss the materials and design of these natural structures.

- Organize the class into pairs, and challenge each pair to design and construct a model canoe. As a class, co-construct criteria for the project, such as:
    - floats in water
    - stays upright
    - does not leak
    - holds a small object

    Provide each student with drawing paper. Have students use applied design, skills, and technologies to plan how to build their model canoe. Have them draw a labelled design and identify the materials they will need to build their canoe.

    Provide access to materials as identified by students. Guide them through the process providing descriptive feedback as appropriate.

    When all pairs have completed their canoes, have them demonstrate the canoes for the class. Discuss various designs and materials and how they met the project criteria.

- Access the interactive activity, Sorting Seats, from the Unit 2 folder in the ***Hands-On Science and Technology, Grade 1*** download. While these interactive activities were originally developed for the Ontario curriculum, they present valuable learning opportunities across grades and provincial curriculums. Find this download at: <https://www.portageandmainpress.com/product/hands-on-interactive-for-science-and-technology-grade-1/>.

Properties of Matter for Grades K–2

8 | How Do We Decide Which Materials Are Best to Do a Job?

Materials

- a story about rain (e.g., *Why Do Puddles Disappear* by Martha Rustad, *The Rainy Day* by Anna Milbourne, *Mud Puddle* by Robert Munsch)
- raincoats, slickers, or ponchos
- rubber boots
- umbrellas
- eyedroppers (one for each working group)
- small containers of water (one for each working group)
- paper towels
- digital cameras (one for each working group)
- materials with varying ability to absorb water (e.g., cotton, rayon, linen, waterproof nylon, plastic) (Label each material by name. Have one sample of each material for each working group.)
- scissors
- glue or clear tape
- chart paper
- markers
- thick paper
- audio-recording device
- Learning-Centre Task Card: How Would You Make a Raincoat? (2.8.1)
- herringbone chart (from lesson 3)

Engage

Read a story about rain to the class. Discuss the story, and ask:

- What do you do to stay dry when it rains?
- How do you dress when it rains?
- Why does the water not go through your raincoat?

Have students examine the raincoats, slickers, or ponchos, the rubber boots, and the umbrellas.

SAFETY NOTE: To avoid injuries, have students examine the umbrellas without opening them.

Ask students:

- What are the materials like for this clothing?
- How are the materials different from the clothing you are wearing now?

Introduce the guided inquiry question: **How do we decide which materials are best to do a job?**

Explore

Organize the class into working groups, and provide each group with samples of materials with varying ability to absorb water (e.g., cotton, rayon, linen, waterproof nylon, plastic). Have groups examine and describe the characteristics of the various materials. Ask the groups to predict and sort the materials according to those that are most likely to let water through and those that are least likely to let water through.

Divide a sheet of chart paper into two columns. Title the first column "Predictions" and the second column "Observations." Record students' predictions in the first column. Introduce the term *absorb*. Explain that when a material absorbs water it means the material soaks up the water. Introduce the term *waterproof*. Explain that when a material does not allow water to soak into or through it, it is called *waterproof*.

Distribute eyedroppers, containers of water, and some paper towels to each group. Give students time to practise using the eyedroppers by having them drop five drops of water from the eyedropper onto a paper towel.

Provide each group with a digital camera to photograph or video record the results of this investigation. Demonstrate use of the camera before they begin.

▶

Now, have students place each cloth sample onto a separate sheet of paper towel. Ask students to squeeze five drops of water onto each sample. Then, tell students to lift the samples to observe the paper towel beneath to see if water leaked through the sample onto the paper towel. Record students' observations on the chart paper in the second column of the chart.

Have students compare their predictions to their observations. Ask:

- Which samples did you think would absorb the most water?
- Which samples absorbed the most water?
- Which samples did you think would absorb only a bit of water?
- Which samples absorbed only a bit of water?
- Which samples did you think would not absorb water?
- Which samples did not absorb water?
- If you had to make your own raincoat or umbrella, which materials would you use?

Have students repeat the water-drop experiment, but this time placing 10 drops of water onto the cloth samples. Again, have students predict, then test to see, if the results from the previous experiment change. Record predictions and observations on chart paper.

Formative Assessment

Observe students as they conduct the water-drop tests. Determine if students are able to:

- safely manipulate materials
- count
- use observation skills
- describe results
- determine the best material for a raincoat or an umbrella

List the criteria on the RUBRIC template on page 53, and record results. Provide descriptive feedback to students about how they met the criteria listed above.

Expand

Provide students with an opportunity to further explore which materials are best to do a specific job by posing their own inquiry questions for personalized learning. They may wish to:

- Initiate a project at the Makerspace centre, such as testing the strength of different brands of garbage bags.
- Explore Loose Parts related to the use of materials with collections of various small fabric swatches (e.g., leather, suede, faux fur). Students can explore the Loose Parts to generate their own inquiry questions.
- Try the water-drop experiment at home (with permission from parents/guardians) to test how other materials absorb water. Students can test objects from around their home (e.g., plastic tumblers, plates, socks, gloves, jeans) then report back to the class.
- Make a commercial to promote the most absorbent material.
- Conduct an investigation or experiment based on their own inquiry questions.

As students explore and select ideas to expand learning, provide support and guidance as needed, and offer access to materials and resources that will enable students to conduct their chosen investigations.

Learning Centre

At the learning centre, provide a variety of fabric samples (including waterproof samples), an audio-recording device, thick paper, scissors, eyedroppers, water, and glue or clear tape, along with a copy of the Learning-Centre Task Card: How Would You Make a Raincoat? (2.8.1):

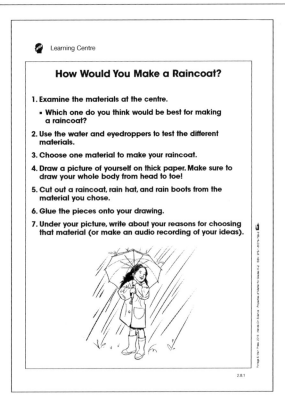

Download this template at <www.portageandmainpress.com/product/HOSMatterK2>.

Have students examine the fabric samples and design a test to determine how waterproof each sample is. They can then select a fabric to make a raincoat. Then, have students draw a picture of themselves on thick paper and cut out fabric to make a raincoat, rain hat, and rain boots from the materials they have selected. Students can glue or tape their rainwear onto their self-portrait, then write about why they chose this material to make a raincoat, or make an audio-recording of their ideas.

Embed Part One: Talking Circle

Revisit the guided inquiry question: **How do we decide which materials are best to do a job?** Have students share their knowledge and experiences, provide examples, and ask further inquiry questions.

Embed Part Two

- Add to the herringbone chart as students learn new concepts, answer some of their own inquiry questions, and ask new inquiry questions.
- Add new terms and illustrations to the word wall. Include the words in languages other than English, such as Indigenous languages, as appropriate.
- Focus on students' use of the Core Competencies. Have students reflect on how they used one of the Core Competencies (Thinking, Communicating, or Personal and Social Skills) during the various lesson activities. Project one of the CORE COMPETENCY DISCUSSION PROMPTS templates (pages 38–42), and use it to inspire group reflection. Referring to the template, choose one or two "I Can" statements on which to focus. Students then use the "I Can" statements to provide evidence of how they demonstrated that competency. Ask questions directly related to that competency to inspire discussion. For example:
  - What are your strengths in learning about materials? (Positive Personal and Cultural Identity)

Have students reflect orally, encouraging participation, questions, and the sharing of evidence (see page 29 for more information on these templates).

As part of this process, students can also set goals. For example, ask:

- What would you do differently next time and why?
- How will you know if you are successful in meeting your goal?
- To encourage self-reflection, provide prompts that students can use to cite examples of

8

how they have used the Core Competencies in their learning. For this purpose, the CORE COMPETENCY SELF-REFLECTION FRAMES (pages 44–47) can be used throughout the learning process. There are five frames provided to address the Core Competencies: Communication, Creative Thinking, Critical Thinking, Positive Personal and Cultural Identity, and Personal Awareness and Responsibility. Conference individually with students to support self-reflection, or students may complete prompts using words and pictures.

Again, have students set goals by considering what they might do differently on future tasks, and how they will know if they are successful in meeting their goal.

NOTE: Use the same prompts from these templates over time to see how thinking changes with different activities.

Enhance

- **Family Connection**: Provide students with one of the following sentence starters:
    - We use waterproof materials at home for _____.
    - We use absorbent materials at home for _____.

  Have students complete their sentence starter at home. Family members can help the student draw and write about this topic. Have students share their sentences with the class.

- Invite a local Elder or Knowledge Keeper to talk about traditional clothing worn in their community, as well as which materials are used and why.

NOTE: See Indigenous Perspectives and Knowledge, page 9, for guidelines for inviting Elders and Knowledge Keepers to speak to students.

- Have students use relevant resources (see Resources for Students, page 67) to research the definitions of related terms (e.g., *waterproof, water-resistant, waterlogged*).

- Create a class book about the water-drop experiment. Have each group write about one material tested and the results. Include their photograph on the page. The first page of the book can be a shared write, in which the class explains to others what they are learning.

- Drain the water from the classroom water table and put a variety of materials and eyedroppers there for continued inquiry and investigation.

- Quick-dry materials allow vapours to freely move through them. Have students examine, then test, a cotton and a quick-dry t-shirt to decide which would be better to wear while exercising on a hot day, and why.

- Read *The Snowy Day* by Ezra Jack Keats, *Sadie and the Snowman* by Allen Morgan or another similar story about snow. Have students observe, compare, and test the insulating properties of several materials. Fill each of four large zipper-lock bags with a different material (e.g., feathers, Styrofoam chips, cotton batting, aluminum foil). Leave a fifth large bag empty. Place four ice cubes into each of five small zipper-lock bags. Seal the bags. Place one small bag containing ice cubes inside each large bag. Try to have about 3 cm of insulating material around the bag with ice cubes. Place the fifth small bag of ice cubes into the last large zipper-lock bag filled with air only, another interesting insulator.

  Have students predict how the outer (large) bags will feel (e.g., cold, warm, hot). After a few minutes, have students feel the outer bags to determine how well the materials are insulating the ice cubes. Leave the bags for

▶

Properties of Matter for Grades K–2

several hours, checking them regularly to see how long it takes the ice cubes in each bag to melt.

NOTE: Use this opportunity to introduce the science concept of *controlling variables*. For students, this will mean making the test as fair as possible. Therefore, it is important to ensure there are equal amounts of materials placed inside each of the large bags, no bag is placed in a sunny or warm location, and the bags are filled at the same time.

- Organize a centre at which students can test the insulating properties of materials. Provide a variety of materials (e.g., shoeboxes, plastic containers, metal containers, fabric samples, cotton batting, wood shavings, shredded paper). Challenge students to design a container that will keep an ice cube frozen for the longest amount of time possible. As a class, co-construct criteria for this challenge. For example:
    - includes recycled materials
    - no larger than a shoebox
    - uses at least three different materials
    - melted ice cube does not leak out of container

    Have each student in the class design and construct an ice-cube keeper. When all ice-cube keepers have been made, have students examine, compare, and contrast them. Also, have students predict which ice-cube keeper will keep an ice cube frozen for the longest period of time. Record students' predictions on chart paper, and set a date for the test. On test day, place an ice cube into each container at the beginning of the day, and check on the ice cubes every hour to determine results. Record these results, and have students infer why some ice-cube keepers worked better than others. Ask:
    - Why do you think the ice cube melted in this ice-cube keeper so quickly?
    - Why do you think this ice-cube keeper kept the ice cube frozen for longer?

    Compare the ice-cube keepers to actual items used to keep food cool (e.g., travel mug, cooler, thermal lunch bag).

- Access the interactive activity, Build a House, from the Unit 2 folder in the ***Hands-On Science and Technology, Grade 1*** download. While these interactive activities were originally developed for the Ontario curriculum, they present valuable learning opportunities across grades and provincial curriculums. Find this download at: <https://www.portageandmainpress.com/product/hands-on-interactive-for-science-and-technology-grade-1/>.

9 Why Is It Important to Choose the Right Material for the Job?

Materials

- *The Three Little Pigs* (several versions)
- straw (dried stalk of grain)
- sticks and twigs
- craft sticks
- LEGO bricks
- bricks
- various items used to join or fasten materials (e.g., stapler and staples, tape, paper clips, string, wool, glue, elastic bands)
- chart paper
- markers
- real-estate advertisements
- drawing paper
- Image Bank: Indigenous Homes (see Appendix, page 175)
- books about Indigenous homes relevant to First Peoples in British Columbia
- projection device (optional)
- pencil crayons
- Learning-Centre Task Card: Buy My House! (2.9.1)
- herringbone chart (from lesson 3)

Engage

Read two or three versions of *The Three Little Pigs* to students. Discuss the story, focusing on the materials the pigs used to build their houses. Discuss the text and illustrations to explore these concepts.

Introduce the guided inquiry question: **Why is it important to choose the right material for the job?**

Explore Part One

Pass around the bricks, straw, sticks and twigs, and craft sticks for students to examine and manipulate. Have them describe the properties of each material.

Ask:

- What does the straw/stick/brick look like?
- What does the straw/stick/brick feel like?
- Does the straw/stick/brick appear to be made of the same material throughout?
- For what do humans use straw/stick/brick?
- From where does straw/stick/brick come?
- How are sticks and twigs the same as craft sticks? How are they different?

Have students share their background knowledge and predictions of where straw and sticks come from, and how bricks are made. As a class, conduct research to answer these questions (see Inquiry Through Research, page 26).

Focus on the houses built by the three pigs in the stories. Ask:

- What objects did the three pigs build?
- Why did the pigs build houses?
- Out of what did the first pig build their house?
- Out of what did the second pig build their house?
- Out of what did the third pig build their house?
- Which pig chose the best material to build their house? Why is it the best material?
- Why could the wolf not blow down the house made of bricks?
- Why do you think the house made from bricks was so strong?
- Why were the houses made of straw and sticks not as strong?
- How do you think the materials used for each house were joined together?

Discuss as a class, and record students' ideas on chart paper.

Explore Part Two

Organize the class into working groups. Explain that each group is going to design and build three houses: one made of straw, one of sticks, and one of LEGO bricks. Before students begin, co-construct criteria for the building project. For example:

- Our house stands on its own.
- Our house fits on an index card (or other predetermined size).
- Our house uses two ways to join materials together.
- We can identify what materials we used to build our house.
- We can explain the reasons why we built our house the way we did.
- I cooperated with the members of my group.

Provide each group with straw, sticks and twigs, LEGO bricks, and various items used to join or fasten materials (e.g., stapler and staples, tape, paper clips, string, wool, glue, elastic bands). Discuss which materials are most sustainable.

As they are building, encourage students to discuss the properties and characteristics of the materials. Encourage students to find ways to fasten the materials together, so the houses are as sturdy as possible. Discuss what may happen if the materials are not fastened properly.

Have each group present its houses to the class. Invite students to discuss the materials they used, the properties of those materials, the fasteners they used, and the sturdiness of their houses. During these presentations, have students identify the sources in nature of some of the materials they used (e.g., straw is the remaining dry stalk of a cereal plant after the grain or seed has been removed, sticks are wood from trees).

Distribute drawing paper to each student, and have students draw a labelled diagram of each of the houses built by their group.

Formative Assessment

Use the RUBRIC template, on page 53, to record whether or not students were able to follow the criteria outlined for the design task. Focus on their ability to transfer and apply learning. Provide descriptive feedback to students about how they chose and used materials, followed criteria, and applied learning.

Explore Part Three

Display the Image Bank: Indigenous Homes. Have students examine and discuss the various homes. Focus on the materials used to build the homes and the designs of each structure.

Invite an Elder or Knowledge Keeper to speak to the class about the homes and other buildings in local Indigenous communities and materials used in their construction.

NOTE: See Indigenous Perspectives and Knowledge, page 9, for guidelines for inviting Elders and Knowledge Keepers to speak to students.

Also read books about Indigenous homes relevant to British Columbia territories, such as:

- *Ch'askin: A Legend of the Sechelt People* by the Sechelt Nation
- *Counting to 100 in the Bighouse* by Pam Holloway

Discuss the different dwellings Indigenous peoples in British Columbia build and the materials (e.g., animal hides, wood from trees) used to build them.

Have students select a dwelling and make a list of materials they would need to build it. Ultimately, this will show them that the materials are from nature, and that people depend on nature for survival. They will also become aware of different cultural perspectives. Encourage students to draw pictures of their selected houses, as well.

NOTE: These modes of construction highlight how Indigenous peoples make use of the available materials. These structures also reflect and determine the nature of social relations in the community.

Expand

Provide students with an opportunity to explore objects and materials further by posing their own inquiry questions for personalized learning. They may wish to:

- Initiate a project at the Makerspace centre, such as using a large refrigerator box to build a playhouse for the classroom. Identify features that the playhouse would need (e.g., door, windows, curtains). Students may also want to include other unique features (e.g., a cozy reading rug, window boxes, carpeting).
- Explore Loose Parts bins related to objects and materials with various small objects made of wood, metal, plastic, and paper, as well as objects made of more than one material. Students can explore the Loose Parts to generate their own inquiry questions.
- Collect pictures of different kinds of homes (e.g., bungalow, two-storey, three-storey, duplex, apartment block, condo). Research the materials used to build each type of housing, as well as the characteristics of each material (see Inquiry Through Research, page 26). This may be an opportunity to connect with a community member in the home construction profession.
- Build model homes using a variety of construction materials (e.g., blocks, straws, connectors, Tinkertoys, Lincoln Logs)

- Conduct an investigation or experiment based on their own inquiry questions.

As students explore and select ideas to expand learning, provide support and guidance as needed, and offer access to materials and resources that will enable students to conduct their chosen investigations.

Learning Centre

At the learning centre, provide real-estate advertisements, several versions of *The Three Little Pigs*, drawing paper, and pencil crayons, along with a copy of the Learning-Centre Task Card: Buy My House! (2.9.1):

Download this template at <www.portageandmainpress.com/product/HOSMatterK2>.

Have students examine the various illustrations of the three little pigs' houses in the books in order to examine and discuss their features. Have them select one house and create an advertisement for it. Discuss the task as a class before students visit the centre, so they understand the importance of promoting the unique characteristics of their selected home in their advertisement (e.g., materials used, size, features).

Embed Part One: Talking Circle

Revisit the guided inquiry question: **Why is it important to choose the right material for the job?** Have students share their knowledge and experiences, provide examples, and ask further inquiry questions.

Embed Part Two

- Add to the herringbone chart as students learn new concepts, answer some of their own inquiry questions, and ask new inquiry questions.
- Add new terms and illustrations to the word wall. Include the words in languages other than English, such as Indigenous languages, as appropriate.
- Focus on students' use of the Core Competencies. Have students reflect on how they used one of the Core Competencies (Thinking, Communicating, or Personal and Social Skills) during the various lesson activities. Project one of the CORE COMPETENCY DISCUSSION PROMPTS templates (pages 38–42), and use it to inspire group reflection. Referring to the template, choose one or two "I Can" statements on which to focus. Students then use the "I Can" statements to provide evidence of how they demonstrated that competency. Ask questions directly related to that competency to inspire discussion. For example:
  - How did you get new ideas about choosing materials for certain jobs? (Critical Thinking)

Have students reflect orally, encouraging participation, questions, and the sharing of evidence (see page 29 for more information on these templates).

As part of this process, students can also set goals. For example, ask:

- What would you do differently next time and why?
- How will you know if you are successful in meeting your goal?

- To encourage self-reflection, provide prompts that students can use to cite examples of how they have used the Core Competencies in their learning. For this purpose, the CORE COMPETENCY SELF-REFLECTION FRAMES (pages 44–47) can be used throughout the learning process. There are five frames provided to address the Core Competencies: Communication, Creative Thinking, Critical Thinking, Positive Personal and Cultural Identity, and Personal Awareness and Responsibility. Conference individually with students to support self-reflection, or students may complete prompts using words and pictures.

Again, have students set goals by considering what they might do differently on future tasks, and how they will know if they are successful in meeting their goal.

NOTE: Use the same prompts from these templates over time to see how thinking changes with different activities.

Enhance

- **Family Connection:** Provide students with the following sentence starter:
  - My home is made of _____.

9

Have students complete the sentence starter at home. Family members can help the student draw and write about this topic. Students may photograph their home to include with their sentence. Have students share their sentences and photograph with the class.

- Take students on a walk around the neighbourhood to look at houses and identify the materials used in the construction of each house. Discuss how materials are joined together (e.g., nails, screws, concrete, mortar, glue).
- Access the interactive activity, Materials Used to Build Playgrounds, from the Unit 2 folder in the **Hands-On Science and Technology, Grade 1** download. While these interactive activities were originally developed for the Ontario curriculum, they present valuable learning opportunities across grades and provincial curriculums. Find this download at: <https://www.portageandmainpress.com/product/hands-on-interactive-for-science-and-technology-grade-1/>.

10 | How Can We Change the Properties of Waste Materials to Use Them in Different Ways?

Materials

- classroom garbage can
- classroom recycling bin
- classroom compost pail
- markers
- chart paper
- Template: Video Viewing Guide (2.10.1)
- computers/tablets with internet access
- projection device
- books by Indigenous authors about respecting the Earth
- poster paper
- art supplies (e.g., crayons, paint, paintbrushes)
- Learning-Centre Task Card: Why Recycle? (2.10.2)
- herringbone chart (from lesson 3)

Engage

Display the classroom garbage can, recycling bin, and compost pail. Ask:

- What kinds of objects do we put in the recycling bin?
- Why do we recycle?
- What kinds of objects do you recycle at home?
- Where do the objects go to be recycled?

Have students share their ideas and background knowledge. Ask:

- What kinds of objects do we put in the garbage can?
- Why do we not recycle these objects?
- What kinds of objects do you put in the garbage bins at home?
- Where do these objects go when they are taken away from the school or your home?

Have students share their ideas and background knowledge. Ask:

- What kinds of objects do we put in the compost pail?
- Why do we compost?
- What kinds of objects do you compost at home?
- What happens to the objects that are composted?
- How do we use the composted materials?

On chart paper, recreate the following chart:

Garbage	Recycling	Compost

Brainstorm a list of objects that are put in the garbage, that are recycled, and that are composted.

Introduce the guided inquiry question: **How can we change the properties of waste materials to use them in different ways?**

Explore Part One

Using the chart created above, have students identify the material from which each waste item is made (e.g., wood, plastic, steel, aluminum, paper, cloth). Also, classify each material as natural (found in nature) or made by humans.

Next, have students watch a video related to reducing, reusing, and recycling. For example:

- "The 3R's for Kids" <https://www.youtube.com/watch?v=TjnNOCbuoCA>
- "Recycle" <https://www.youtube.com/watch?v=BaFpv03hq-4>

Before watching the video, project the Template: Video Viewing Guide (2.10.1):

10

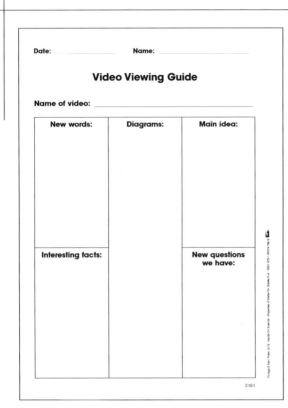

Download this template at <www.portageandmainpress.com/product/HOSMatterK2>.

Review the headings with students. Explain that the class will complete the guide together after watching the video.

After watching the video, complete as a class the Template: Video Viewing Guide (2.10.1). Focus discussion on the reasons why waste needs to be reduced and on the importance of recycling.

Explore Part Two

Construct a tally chart near the classroom garbage can and recycling bin. Have students add a tick to the chart each time they place an item in either bin.

Present data with pictographs or bar graphs, to compare daily amounts of waste.

Explore Part Three

As a class, brainstorm ways to reduce the amount of waste produced in the classroom, both garbage and recycled materials. Be sure to have students explain why each action is important. Record these ideas on chart paper.

Select one idea as a class action-plan project. Post your plan clearly for all students to see, and share it with others in the school. For the rest of the school year, remind students of this plan.

Explore Part Four

Have students explore how Indigenous peoples show their respect for their environment and their natural resources. For example, when they hunt and harvest animals, they do not take just the meat for food. They use all parts of the animal. Black bears are important to many groups in British Columbia. The meat can be preserved and the fur can also be used. The fat under the skin can be conserved as a spread or for personal use. Teeth and bones can be used for jewellery or tools. Some communities use everything aside from the liver. Invite a local Elder or Knowledge Keeper to present to the class about reducing waste, or as a class, conduct research to explore these forms of reducing waste.

NOTE: See Indigenous Perspectives and Knowledge, page 9, for guidelines for inviting Elders and Knowledge Keepers to speak to students.

Invite a local Elder or Knowledge Keeper to discuss the respect Indigenous peoples have for the Earth. Then, read books such as:

- *Taking Care of Our Mother Earth* by Celestine Aleck
- *Lessons From Mother Earth* by Elaine McLeod
- *Talking With Mother Earth* by Jorge Argueta

Presentations and literature connections may help students understand that littering and pollution are not respectful of Mother Earth. They may be encouraged and inspired to take local actions (e.g., clean up the school yard, share the message with the whole school, organize a community clean-up).

Expand

Provide students with an opportunity to explore waste materials further by posing their own inquiry questions for personalized learning. They may wish to:

- Initiate a project at the Makerspace centre, such as using a large refrigerator box to build a playhouse for the classroom. Identify features that a playhouse needs (e.g., door, windows, curtains). Students may also want to include unique features (e.g., cozy reading rug, window boxes, carpeting).
- Explore Loose Parts bins with various small objects made of wood, metal, plastic, paper, as well as objects made of more than one material. Students can explore the Loose Parts to generate their own inquiry questions.
- Research and set up a vermicomposter (worm composter) in the classroom to compost lunch waste. Use the resulting materials for garden or plant fertilizer (see Inquiry Through Research, page 26).
- Start a recycling project (e.g., collect plastic bags to make into Frisbees).
- Propose and promote a litterless lunch day each week.
- Save paper from the class recycling bin and use it to make recycled paper, greeting cards, or bookmarks.
- Assess, and then propose improvements to, the current recycling and garbage system in your school.
- Make commercials to promote the use of fabric grocery bags instead of plastic bags.
- Conduct an investigation or experiment based on their own inquiry questions.

As students explore and select ideas to expand learning, provide support and guidance as needed, and offer access to materials and resources that will enable students to conduct their chosen investigations.

Learning Centre

At the learning centre, provide poster paper and art supplies (e.g., crayons, paint, paintbrushes), along with a copy of the Learning-Centre Task Card: Why Recycle? (2.10.2):

Download this template at <www.portageandmainpress.com/product/HOSMatterK2>.

Have students work together to reflect on why it is important to use recycled materials, and what could happen to Earth if humans used only new materials and did not recycle. Have them work in pairs or groups to create a poster to promote recycling.

Student Self-Assessment

Focus on taking part in caring for self, family, and community. Have students take home a copy of the FAMILY AND COMMUNITY CONNECTIONS: ASSESSING TOGETHER template on page 57. Have them complete the template with a family or community member (with permission) to reflect on their learning about waste and recycling.

Embed Part One: Talking Circle

Revisit the guided inquiry question: **How can we change the properties of waste materials to use them in different ways?** Have students share their knowledge and experiences, provide examples, and ask further inquiry questions.

Embed Part Two

- Add to the herringbone chart as students learn new concepts, answer some of their own inquiry questions, and ask new inquiry questions.
- Add new terms and illustrations to the word wall. Include the words in languages other than English, such as Indigenous languages, as appropriate.
- Focus on students' use of the Core Competencies. Have students reflect on how they used one of the Core Competencies (Thinking, Communicating, or Personal and Social Skills) during the various lesson activities. Project one of the CORE COMPETENCY DISCUSSION PROMPTS templates (pages 38–42), and use it to inspire group reflection. Referring to the template, choose one or two "I Can" statements on which to focus. Students then use the "I Can" statements to provide evidence of how they demonstrated that competency. Ask questions directly related to that competency to inspire discussion. For example:

- How did you share your learning with others today? (Communication)

Have students reflect orally, encouraging participation, questions, and the sharing of evidence (see page 29 for more information on these templates).

As part of this process, students can also set goals. For example, ask:

- What would you do differently next time and why?
- How will you know if you are successful in meeting your goal?

- To encourage self-reflection, provide prompts that students can use to cite examples of how they have used the Core Competencies in their learning. For this purpose, the CORE COMPETENCY SELF-REFLECTION FRAMES (pages 44–47) can be used throughout the learning process. There are five frames provided to address the Core Competencies: Communication, Creative Thinking, Critical Thinking, Positive Personal and Cultural Identity, and Personal Awareness and Responsibility. Conference individually with students to support self-reflection, or students may complete prompts using words and pictures.

Again, have students set goals by considering what they might do differently on future tasks, and how they will know if they are successful in meeting their goal.

NOTE: Use the same prompts from these templates over time to see how thinking changes with different activities.

Enhance

- **Family Connection:** Provide students with the following sentence starter:
  - We recycle at home by _____.

▶

- Have students complete the sentence starter at home. Family members can help the student draw and write about this topic.
- Challenge students and their families to measure how much recycled materials they collect in a week. This might involve using standard measures (weighing recycled materials) or nonstandard measures (number of bins/bags). Recycled materials can also be sorted (e.g., cans, plastics, paper) and measured to compare how much of each is collected.
- Take a guided field trip to a landfill or a recycling depot. Metro Vancouver offers these tours to school groups.
- Introduce students to the following visual for *Reduce, Reuse, Recycle*:

There are many different versions of this visual. Challenge students to create their own visual that promotes the process. This is an opportunity to learn about the cyclical pattern so that students can be more environmentally conscious in the decisions they make on a daily basis.

- Introduce students to *middens*—waste areas that tell a great deal about past generations and human history. Archaeologists love discovering middens because they tell us so much about the people who made them and their lives. Shell middens, for example, are believed to be the remains of hunting and nomadic groups feeding on mollusks in coastal areas. The shell midden in Namu, British Columbia is over nine metres deep and is over 10,000 years old. Ask students:
  - What would future generations or aliens infer about us from what we throw out?
- Does everyone in the world have the same garbage?
- Watch the National Geographic series *Trashopolis*, which shows how different large cities (e.g., Montreal, Paris, Rome, Tokyo, Los Angeles) tackle their trash.
- Access the interactive activity, Sorting Classroom Waste, from the Unit 2 folder in the **Hands-On Science and Technology, Grade 1** download. While these interactive activities were originally developed for the Ontario curriculum, they present valuable learning opportunities across grades and provincial curriculums. Find this download at: <https://www.portageandmainpress.com/product/hands-on-interactive-for-science-and-technology-grade-1/>.

11 | How Can We Use Materials in Different Ways to Design and Construct Objects?

Materials

- several large boxes or bins (for storing sorted recyclable items)
- Learning-Centre Task Card: Constructing a Treasure Box (2.11.1)
- digital camera
- small cardboard boxes
- art supplies (e.g., crayons, paint, paintbrushes)
- scissors
- glue
- variety of objects to use as fasteners (e.g., buttons, string, pipe cleaners, Velcro)
- egg cartons*
- Styrofoam trays, plates, cups*
- plastic and paper bags*
- boxes*
- plastic pop bottles*
- milk jugs*
- newspapers*
- wrapping paper*
- cardboard milk cartons*
- margarine tubs and other plastic food containers*
- cardboard rolls (from toilet paper or paper towels)*
- items determined by students after planning their projects (e.g., clear tape, masking tape, glue, paint, aluminum foil, sparkles)
- herringbone chart (from lesson 3)

*NOTE: This lesson presents an opportunity for students to learn about recycling by having them collect recyclables from home. Send a note home to parents/guardians explaining the project, and ask them to help provide clean recyclable materials.

Engage

As students bring recyclable items to school, have them sort the items by type of material into the large boxes. When there is a sufficient quantity and variety, display the items for students to examine.

Ask:

- From where did these objects come?
- Why did you not just throw the objects in the garbage?
- Why is it important to reuse and recycle?
- How does reusing and recycling help us?
- How does reusing and recycling help the environment?

Introduce the guided inquiry question: **How can we use materials in different ways to design and construct objects?**

Explore Part One

Explain to students that they are going to make a new object from the materials collected. Have students brainstorm things they could make. Encourage students to make lists according to various functions, in order to identify the purpose for their creation. For example:

- items to hold things in the classroom:
    - pencil holder
    - crayon box
    - desk organizer
    - book/magazine holder
- items for play:
    - boat
    - car
    - toy animal or doll
    - rocket
    - spaceship
    - robot
    - character(s) from books
    - doll or model furniture
- items that help another living thing:
    - bird feeder
    - birdhouse
    - butterfly house

▶

- bat house
- ladybug house

NOTE: Refer to children's craft books for further ideas on items to make.

When students have decided what they will build, organize the class into groups of students who are building similar items. Meet with each group, and discuss criteria for students' projects. Ensure the criteria includes identifying the function or purpose of the object. Distribute paper to each student to record the criteria.

Explore Part Two

Have students plan and design their projects. Have them record the type of object they are going to build, what the object will be used for, and why they have chosen to build it. Also, have them list the materials they will need for construction. Give students plenty of time to think about the criteria, as well as time to plan and design their object. Have students draw a diagram of their design, and discuss how they might use the various recycled materials collected to build their items (e.g., a boat could be made from a milk carton, with a straw and a piece of cardboard for the sail; a rocket could be made from cardboard rolls; a bird feeder could be made from a clear pop bottle). As a class, discuss any other things students will need to complete their projects. Be sure students address how to fasten materials together, and how to decorate.

Formative Assessment

Before students begin the construction process, conference with them individually to discuss their ideas for their object, design, and materials, and how they plan to meet the criteria. Focus on their ability to generate and introduce new or refined ideas during this design task. Use the INDIVIDUAL STUDENT OBSERVATIONS template, on page 51, to record results. Provide descriptive feedback to students about how they generated new ideas to use specific materials in the construction of their chosen object.

Explore Part Three

Collaborate with students to determine a date to complete their projects. When they have completed their projects, have them present their project to the class. Have students discuss their design and completed project with classmates, receive peer feedback, and assess if the design has met the project criteria.

Summative Assessment

Use a digital camera to photograph students with their completed projects. Include these in their science portfolio (see The **Hands-On Science** Assessment Plan, page 29, for information about student portfolios and portfolio templates). Use the portfolio to provide descriptive feedback on how students demonstrate:

- curiosity and a sense of wonder about their science learning
- understanding of the characteristics of materials used in the construction of their projects

Expand

Provide students with an opportunity to explore objects and materials further by posing their own inquiry questions for personalized learning. They may wish to:

- Initiate a project at the Makerspace centre, such as designing and constructing an object from recycled materials related to a special interest or hobby (e.g., a mini floor hockey net, a pup tent for camping).
- Explore Loose Parts related to recycling with collections of various small recycled objects (e.g., cardboard tubes, plastic and metal lids, tin cans [with any sharp edges covered or

▶

filed]). Students can explore the Loose Parts to generate their own inquiry questions.
- Construct another object, based on classmates' projects
- Conduct an investigation or experiment based on their own inquiry questions.

As students explore and select ideas to expand learning, provide support and guidance as needed, and offer access to materials and resources that will enable students to conduct their chosen investigations.

Learning Centre

At the learning centre, provide small cardboard boxes, scissors, glue, art supplies (e.g., crayons, paint, paintbrushes), and a variety of objects to use as fasteners (e.g., buttons, string, pipe cleaners, Velcro), along with a copy of the Learning-Centre Task Card: Constructing a Treasure Box (2.11.1):

Download this template at <www.portageandmainpress.com/product/HOSMatterK2>.

Have students construct treasure boxes to hold special collections (e.g., hockey cards, shells, rocks, coins).

Embed Part One: Talking Circle

Revisit the guided inquiry question: **How can we use materials in different ways to design and construct objects?** Have students share their knowledge and experiences, provide examples, and ask further inquiry questions.

Embed Part Two

- Add to the herringbone chart as students learn new concepts, answer some of their own inquiry questions, and ask new inquiry questions.
- Add new terms and illustrations to the word wall. Include the words in languages other than English, such as Indigenous languages, as appropriate.
- Focus on students' use of the Core Competencies. Have students reflect on how they used one of the Core Competencies (Thinking, Communicating, or Personal and Social Skills) during the various lesson activities. Project one of the CORE COMPETENCY DISCUSSION PROMPTS templates (pages 38–42), and use it to inspire group reflection. Referring to the template, choose one or two "I Can" statements on which to focus. Students then use the "I Can" statements to provide evidence of how they demonstrated that competency. Ask questions directly related to that competency to inspire discussion. For example:
  - How do you feel about recycling? Why is it important to you? (Positive Personal and Cultural Identity)

Properties of Matter for Grades K–2

11

Have students reflect orally, encouraging participation, questions, and the sharing of evidence (see page 29 for more information on these templates). As part of this process, students can also set goals. For example, ask:

- What would you do differently next time and why?
- How will you know if you are successful in meeting your goal?

■ To encourage self-reflection, provide prompts that students can use to cite examples of how they have used the Core Competencies in their learning. For this purpose, the CORE COMPETENCY SELF-REFLECTION FRAMES (pages 44–47) can be used throughout the learning process. There are five frames provided to address the Core Competencies: Communication, Creative Thinking, Critical Thinking, Positive Personal and Cultural Identity, and Personal Awareness and Responsibility. Conference individually with students to support self-reflection, or students may complete prompts using words and pictures.

Again, have students set goals by considering what they might do differently on future tasks, and how they will know if they are successful in meeting their goal.

NOTE: Use the same prompts from these templates over time to see how thinking changes with different activities.

Enhance

- **Family Connection**: Provide students with the following sentence starter:
    - We can make a useful object from recycled materials at home, such as _____.

  Have students complete the sentence starter at home. Family members can help draw

and write about this topic, and construct an object from recycled materials together. Encourage students to bring these objects back to school to share with the class.

■ Keep a big box in the classroom for collecting recycled materials. As an ongoing, year-long activity, have students use the materials to build items at a construction centre or the Makerspace centre.

■ Access the interactive activity, Building From Recycled Materials, from the Unit 2 folder in the ***Hands-On Science and Technology, Grade 1*** download. While these interactive activities were originally developed for the Ontario curriculum, they present valuable learning opportunities across grades and provincial curriculums. Find this download at: <https://www.portageandmainpress.com/product/hands-on-interactive-for-science-and-technology-grade-1/>.

12 | What Do We Know About Solids and Liquids?

Information for Teachers

Matter is any substance that has mass and takes up space. Matter comes in different forms and is classified into three states: *solids*, *liquids*, and *gases*. (A fourth state of matter called *plasma* is beyond the scope of kindergarten to grade 2.) Molecules in solids, liquids, and gases vibrate.

Molecules in solids are attracted to each other and are packed close together, so solids retain their shape and volume. Solids can be broken, but are not very compressible due to the rigid and close arrangement of their particles.

Molecules in liquids are also attracted to each other but can overcome the attraction enough to collide and flow. This means they are also not very compressible. As a result, liquids have a definite volume and take the shape of their container. Liquids can be poured and can often splash and form droplets.

Molecules in gases have less attraction and lots of free space between particles. Relative to liquids and solids, molecules in gases move quickly, and collide more often. Gases do not have a fixed shape, and they expand to fill the space they are in. They are also compressible due to the large amount of space between particles.

NOTE: The term *molecule* is not used in the curriculum at this level, but may be introduced to aid explanations.

Materials

- plastic or cloth bags (one for each student)
- sticky notes
- soft butter
- markers
- chart paper
- digital camera
- place-based journals and supplies
- *Cloudwalker* by Roy Henry Vickers and Robert Budd
- "lab" coats (e.g., repurposed adult-size white shirts)
- map of local area
- map of traditional territories of First Peoples in British Columbia (see lesson 1)

Engage

Have students imagine themselves as well-known scientists who are going on a scavenger hunt. To help them prepare for the role of scientist, have students put on a "lab" coat. Provide each student with a plastic or cloth bag.

On chart paper, record a list of items each student scientist should try to find:

- something soft
- something that rolls
- something made of metal

Give students a few minutes to hunt for these items in the classroom. Have them put the items they find into their bags.

Next, have students return to their seats, and give each student three sticky notes. Ask them to record or draw each item in their bag on a separate sticky note.

NOTE: Keep these sticky notes for the next activity.

Have students look at their items. Ask:

- What did you find?
- How can you describe one of your objects?

Have students share descriptions of their items. Ask:

- What do your items have in common?
- Are they all solids?
- How do you know which items are solids?
- Are any of the objects liquids?

12

Introduce the guided inquiry question: **What do we know about solids and liquids?**

Explore Part One

On chart paper, begin constructing a concept web, adding the sticky notes from the Engage task, as in the following example:

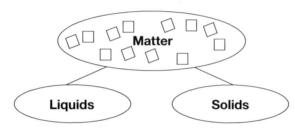

Now, discuss students' background knowledge of solids and liquids. Ask:

- What do you know about liquids?
- What are some examples of liquids?

Record students' ideas by adding them to the concept web. Repeat this process for solids.

Next, provide each student with three more sticky notes. Ask them to record, on each sticky note, one question they have about solids and liquids. To trigger questions, display the soft butter. Ask:

- What questions can you ask about butter?

Some example questions could be:

- Is butter a solid or a liquid?
- Can butter be changed from a solid into a liquid?

NOTE: If students created the ice cube keepers in lesson 8, remind them of this task and discuss what changes they observed in the ice cube.

Have students generate their own questions about anything related to solids and liquids. Sort students' sticky notes according to questions related to solids or liquids, and add them to the concept web.

Display this concept web in a visible area of the classroom for students to reference throughout the module.

Explore Part Two

Plan a nature walk to the location visited in lesson 1.

NOTE: Revisiting the same place builds a connection to the land, which encourages students to protect it. This incorporates concepts from the First Peoples Principles of Learning related to supporting the well-being of the land and developing a sense of place, connectedness, and reciprocal relationships.

Consider inviting a local Elder or Knowledge Keeper to guide the nature walk to share knowledge or stories about solids and liquids.

NOTE: See Indigenous Perspectives and Knowledge, page 9, for guidelines for inviting Elders and Knowledge Keepers to speak to students.

Before the walk, be sure to review with students the importance of being respectful of nature when collecting objects. Review the anchor chart created in lesson 1.

As with all place-based learning activities:

- Identify the importance of place. Use a map of the local area to identify where the location is in relation to the school.
- Identify on whose traditional territory the school is located, as well as the traditional territory of the location for the nature walk, if different.
- Incorporate land acknowledgment using local protocols.

Review any other protocols for field trips, providing students with opportunities to ask questions and clarify expectations. Also, review safety issues (e.g., take care when collecting objects that may have sharp edges).

Have students share with a partner what they are most excited about in visiting this location for place-based learning.

Have students look for examples and evidence of solids (e.g., rocks, shells, sticks, soil, trees, grass) and liquids (e.g., puddles, ponds, streams, rain, sap) in the natural environment.

Use a digital camera to photograph students' examples for use back in the classroom. Artifacts may be collected to display in the classroom, or to use for subsequent sorting activities.

Hand out place-based journals and supplies. As a class, choose a place to sit and journal. Brainstorm journaling ideas related to solids and liquids in the natural environment. For example, at the kindergarten to grade-two level, students may want to:

- sketch and colour solids and/or liquids in a natural setting
- identify emotions and record feelings about solids and/or liquids (students may use happy faces, emojis, or their own designs for emojis)
- take a photograph that shows characteristics of a solid or liquid and sketch it
- draw labelled diagrams showing solids and/or liquids
- use all the senses to describe solids and/or liquids using pictures

Explore Part Three

With the class, complete a book walk using *Cloudwalker* by Roy Henry Vickers and Robert Budd. This Gitxsan story about weather, river ecology, water cycle, identity, and community is suitable for prereaders or emergent readers.

NOTE: See lesson 2 for more information about book walks.

Expand

Provide students with an opportunity to explore solids and liquids further by posing their own inquiry questions for personalized learning. They may wish to:

- Initiate a project at the Makerspace centre, such as designing and constructing a boat that floats in water.
- Explore Loose Parts bins related to flotation with a variety of small objects that float and objects that sink (e.g., wooden and plastic thread spools, broken crayons, buttons, Styrofoam chips, wooden dowels, wooden shims, marbles). Students can explore the Loose Parts to generate their own inquiry questions.
- Take photographs of solids and liquids at home and create a graphic organizer to sort them.
- Sort liquids by properties (e.g., colour, thickness, use) and graph results.
- Conduct an investigation or experiment based on their own inquiry questions.

As students explore and select ideas to expand learning, provide support and guidance as needed, and offer access to materials and resources that will enable students to conduct their chosen investigations.

Embed Part One: Talking Circle

Revisit the guided inquiry question: **What do we know about solids and liquids?** Have students share their knowledge and experiences, provide examples, and ask further inquiry questions.

Embed Part Two

- Add to the concept web as students learn new concepts, answer some of their own inquiry questions, and ask new inquiry questions.

12

- Add new terms and illustrations to the word wall. Include the words in languages other than English, such as Indigenous languages, as appropriate.
- Focus on students' use of the Core Competencies. Have students reflect on how they used one of the Core Competencies (Thinking, Communicating, or Personal and Social Skills) during the various lesson activities. Project one of the CORE COMPETENCY DISCUSSION PROMPTS templates (pages 38–42), and use it to inspire group reflection. Referring to the template, choose one or two "I Can" statements on which to focus. Students then use the "I Can" statements to provide evidence of how they demonstrated that competency. Ask questions directly related to that competency to inspire discussion. For example:
    - How did you get new ideas as you learned today? (Creative Thinking)

  Have students reflect orally, encouraging participation, questions, and the sharing of evidence (see page 29 for more information on these templates).
  As part of this process, students can also set goals. For example, ask:
    - What would you do differently next time and why?
    - How will you know if you are successful in meeting your goal?
- To encourage self-reflection, provide prompts that students can use to cite examples of how they have used the Core Competencies in their learning. For this purpose, the CORE COMPETENCY SELF-REFLECTION FRAMES (pages 44–47) can be used throughout the learning process. There are five frames provided to address the Core Competencies: Communication, Creative Thinking, Critical Thinking, Positive Personal and Cultural Identity, and Personal Awareness and Responsibility. Conference individually with students to support self-reflection, or students may complete prompts using words and pictures.

  Again, have students set goals by considering what they might do differently on future tasks and how they will know if they are successful in meeting their goal.

NOTE: Use the same prompts from these templates over time to see how thinking changes with different activities.

Enhance

- **Family Connection**: Provide students with the following sentence starter:
    - Some solids and liquids in our home are _____.

  Have students complete the sentence starter at home. Family members can help the student draw and write about this topic. Extend the task by having students and their families identify common characteristics of solid or liquids. For example:
    - These solids are all the same because _____.
    - These liquids are all the same because _____.

  Have students share their sentences with the class.

13 What Are Solids and Liquids?

Materials

- water bottle, filled and capped
- two empty jars
- chart paper
- markers
- clear plastic containers or jars with lids, filled with liquids (e.g., water, dish soap, syrup, vinegar, oil) (Label each jar with the name of the liquid.)
- clear plastic containers or jars with lids, filled with small solid items (e.g., buttons, stones, erasers, coins, nails, washers, tiles) (Label each jar with the name of the solid.)
- variety of solids (e.g., building blocks, LEGO, books, pencils, crayons)
- magnifying glasses
- glue
- scissors
- computer/tablet with internet access
- writing paper
- Learning-Centre Task Card: Sorting and Graphing Solids and Liquids (2.13.1)
- Learning-Centre Template: Sorting and Graphing Solids and Liquids (2.13.2)
- Learning-Centre Template: Pictograph Symbols (2.13.3)
- sticky notes
- concept web (from lesson 12)

Engage

Give students 30 seconds to search the classroom for an item they are able to hold in one hand.

Have each student display their item and explain of what the object is made. Ask:

- Are all these objects solids?
- Are any items liquids?
- How do you know?

Now, display the filled water bottle. Ask:

- What is inside this bottle?
- Is water a solid or a liquid?
- How do you know water is a liquid?

Have students share their ideas.

Introduce the guided inquiry question: **What are solids and liquids?**

Explore Part One

Organize the class into working groups. Provide each group with a variety of solids and liquids (e.g., building blocks, LEGO, books, pencils, crayons; jars containing water, dish soap, vinegar, oil). Allow students time to manipulate and discuss the materials. Then, ask:

- How can you sort these items into groups?

Construct a sorting mat on chart paper:

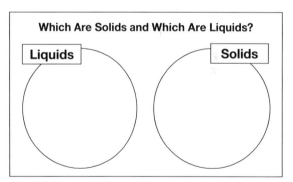

Provide each group with chart paper and markers. Have groups construct their own sorting mat, and use it to record their sorting (sorting mats can be co-constructed as a class, or groups can be supported with adult supervision if needed). Students may use the terms *solid* and *liquid* as their sorting rules, or they may use "liquid" and "not liquid" or "solid" and "not solid."

Explore Part Two

As a class, discuss the sorting activity. Ask:

- How did you sort the items?

- If you identified some of the objects as solids, how do you know they are solids?
- How are solids different from liquids?

Demonstrate the properties of solids by having students stack (or pile up) solid objects. Place a solid object into one empty jar, and pour a liquid into another empty jar. Ask:

- How are solids and liquids different from each other?
- How are solids and liquids similar to each other?

Connect the activity to what students know about the senses. Ask:

- What does your sense of sight tell you about solids?
- Can you hear a liquid? (when it is being poured, splashed, or swished)
- Which liquids can you smell?
- Which solids feel rough? sharp? soft?

Divide a sheet of chart paper into two columns. Title the first column "Solids." Have students brainstorm a list of solids, and record these in the first column. Title the second column "Properties of Solids." Discuss the term *property* as another word for *characteristic*. Have students describe, in their own words, some of the properties of solids.

On another sheet of chart paper, make two columns. Title the first column "Liquids" and have students brainstorm a list of liquids. Ask students to describe which liquids they use in their homes, and how they use them.

Title the second column "Properties of Liquids." Have students describe, in their own words, some of the properties of liquids.

Display these charts in the classroom throughout the rest of the module to help students identify different types of matter.

Explore Part Three

Have students learn about igloos as a means of exploring the solid state of water. Igloos are made of compacted snow, use a dome shape for strength, and use a rising spiral for construction purposes. The following video, "How To Build An Igloo | A Boy Among Polar Bears | BBC," shows an Inuit boy building an igloo: <https://www.youtube.com/watch?v=R-x5QOSqP3E>.

After watching the video, pose the following questions for review and further inquiry:

- Why is snow better than ice for building an igloo?
- Why do you use a circle for the shape?
- Why do you use a rising spiral pattern to build the igloo?
- How does the dome shape make the igloo strong?
- How does an igloo—made of snow—allow those inside to stay warm?

For further exploration of snow, consider the following questions:

- What type of snow is best for making snowballs? Snowmen?
- When does snow squeak and why?
- Does snow have to melt to disappear?

Expand

Provide students with an opportunity to explore solids and liquids further by posing their own inquiry questions for personalized learning. They may wish to:

- Initiate a project at the Makerspace centre, such as designing and constructing a device to clean dirty water.
- Explore Loose Parts related to solids and liquids. For example, fill baby food jars with a variety of liquids and solids. Students can explore the Loose Parts to generate their own inquiry questions.

▶

13

- Photograph solids and liquids at home and create a graphic organizer to sort them.
- Sort liquids by properties (e.g., colour, thickness, use) and graph results.
- Conduct an investigation or experiment based on their own inquiry questions.

NOTE: Ensure sand and water tables are available to further explore solids and liquids.

As students explore and select ideas to expand learning, provide support and guidance as needed, and offer access to materials and resources that will enable students to conduct their chosen investigations.

Learning Centre

At the learning centre, provide several clear plastic containers or jars (labelled, with lids) filled with liquids (e.g., water, dish soap, syrup, vinegar, oil) and several clear plastic containers or jars (labelled, with lids) filled with small solid items (e.g., buttons, stones, erasers, coins, nails, washers, tiles). Also, provide magnifying glasses, glue, scissors, writing paper, a copy of the Learning-Centre Task Card: Sorting and Graphing Solids and Liquids (2.13.1), copies of the Learning-Centre Template: Sorting and Graphing Solids and Liquids (2.13.2), and copies of the Learning-Centre Template: Pictograph Symbols (2.13.3):

13

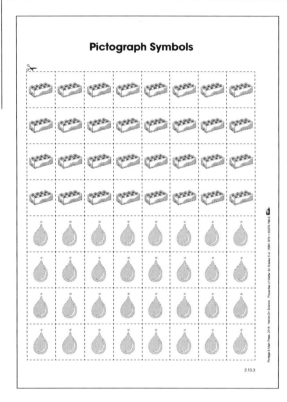

Download these templates at <www.portageandmainpress.com/product/HOSMatterK2>.

Have students record on the template (2.13.2) the name of each item (both solids and liquids). Then have them examine each item, and identify, with a check mark, if the item is a solid or a liquid. Finally, ask students to count the number of jars of solids and liquids and create a pictograph of their results using the pictograph symbols (2.13.3).

Embed Part One: Talking Circle

Revisit the guided inquiry question: **What are solids and liquids?** Have students share their knowledge and experiences, provide examples, and ask further inquiry questions.

Embed Part Two

- Add to the concept web as students learn new concepts, answer some of their own inquiry questions, and ask new inquiry questions.
- Add new terms and illustrations to the word wall. Include the words in languages other than English, such as Indigenous languages, as appropriate.
- Focus on students' use of the Core Competencies. Have students reflect on how they used one of the Core Competencies (Thinking, Communicating, or Personal and Social Skills) during the various lesson activities. Project one of the CORE COMPETENCY DISCUSSION PROMPTS templates (pages 38–42), and use it to inspire group reflection. Referring to the template, choose one or two "I Can" statements on which to focus. Students then use the "I Can" statements to provide evidence of how they demonstrated that competency. Ask questions directly related to that competency to inspire discussion. For example:
  - How did you explore materials to learn about solids and liquids today? (Critical Thinking)

Have students reflect orally, encouraging participation, questions, and the sharing of evidence (see page 29 for more information on these templates).

As part of this process, students can also set goals. For example, ask:

- What would you do differently next time and why?
- How will you know if you are successful in meeting your goal?
- To encourage self-reflection, provide prompts that students can use to cite examples of how they have used the Core Competencies in their learning. For this purpose, the

132   Hands-On Science: An Inquiry Approach • Grades K–2

CORE COMPETENCY SELF-REFLECTION FRAMES (pages 44–47) can be used throughout the learning process. There are five frames provided to address the Core Competencies: Communication, Creative Thinking, Critical Thinking, Positive Personal and Cultural Identity, and Personal Awareness and Responsibility. Conference individually with students to support self-reflection, or students may complete prompts using words and pictures.

Again, have students set goals by considering what they might do differently on future tasks, and how they will know if they are successful in meeting their goal.

NOTE: Use the same prompts from these templates over time to see how thinking changes with different activities.

Formative Assessment

Through individual conferences, have students sort a variety of objects as solids and liquids. Ask them to explain the properties of each. Have students provide additional examples of both solids and liquids from everyday life. Focus on their ability to observe the properties of matter in familiar contexts. Use the INDIVIDUAL STUDENT OBSERVATIONS template, on page 51, to record results. Provide descriptive feedback to students about how they observe and explain the properties of materials.

Enhance

- **Family Connection**: Provide students with the following sentence starter:
    - Three examples of solids and liquids in our neighbourhood are _____.

    Have students complete the sentence starter at home. Family members can help students draw and write about this topic. Have students share their sentences with the class.

- Many students may believe a solid object is always hard. In fact, many solids, when in very small pieces, can be poured like liquids. Although solids like sand and sugar take the shape of their container, they also tend to stack up when they are poured onto a flat surface, whereas liquids spread out into a thin layer. Have students work with a variety of solids (e.g., salt, sugar, sand, uncooked rice, aluminum foil, beads). Each will, generally, take on the shape of its container. Have students use a magnifying glass to examine the "small pieces." They may notice there is space between the small solid pieces, which retain their shape. When students examine liquid through a magnifying glass, they will not find spaces. Pose a question to turn this into a short, independent inquiry. For example:
    - Is sugar/salt/sand a solid or a liquid?

    Students can explore the substance, design their own inquiry, and come up with an answer, supported by evidence.

- Have students learn more about the characteristics of solids by manipulating and changing them, while also making aesthetically pleasing products. For this activity, you will need the following materials:
    - chalk (various colours)
    - something to crush chalk (e.g., mortar and pestle, small rock, ice cream scoop, heavy spoon)
    - small, narrow jar with lid
    - salt
    - bowl

    Have students place a handful of salt and a piece of chalk in a bowl, then grind the chalk into the salt until it produces the desired colour. Students can pour the coloured salt into the jar, and then colour other batches of salt to add to the jar. Have students tilt the jar or stir the contents with a pencil to

13

create interesting designs in the coloured salt. To prevent the salt from shfiting, ensure students' jars are filled to the top with the lids tightly secured.

- With permission from parents/guardians, have students investigate solids and liquids in their homes—in refrigerators and cupboards. Encourage them to find ways to sort and record their findings.

- Access the interactive activity, Solids & Liquids, from the Unit 3 folder in the ***Hands-On Science and Technology, Grade 2*** download. While these interactive activities were originally developed for the Ontario curriculum, they present valuable learning opportunities across grades and provincial curriculums. Find this download at: <https://www.portageandmainpress.com/product/hands-on-interactive-for-science-and-technology-grade-2/>.

14 | What Are Some Properties of Liquids?

Information for Teachers

A *property* is a distinctive characteristic or attribute. Some properties of liquids students will explore in this lesson include:

- *transparent*: easily seen through because light is transmitted through it
- *translucent*: allows light through, but diffuses the light, so visibility is limited
- *opaque*: does not allow light to pass through
- *viscosity*: extent to which a fluid flows, or its thickness
- *absorbency*: ability of a solid to soak up a liquid

SAFETY NOTE: Activities in this lesson require the use of various liquids. Do not use liquids that are unsafe to taste, smell, or touch, and check students' medical files for any allergies.

Before beginning this lesson, create the following three classroom reference posters on chart paper. Display actual materials on the posters as examples, when possible.

Poster 1: Transparency

Title the poster "Transparency." Record the term *translucent* in large letters under the title. Next to the word, cut a window in the paper. Tape a piece of wax paper to the back of the chart paper to show through the window.

Record the term *transparent* in large letters. Next to the word, cut another window, this time taping a piece of plastic wrap to the back of the chart paper.

Record the term *opaque*; cut a third window, and tape a piece of construction paper to the back of the chart paper.

Poster 2: Viscosity

Title the poster "Viscosity." Under the title, draw each of the terms *thick*, *thin*, *oozing* and *runny* the way they look. For example:

Photographs of liquids of varying viscosities may also be included on the poster.

Poster 3: Absorption

Title the poster "Absorption." Dip materials (e.g., paper towels, coffee filters, vinyl tablecloth, various fabrics) into food colouring to show absorbency.

Use material that shows no absorption (e.g., piece of vinyl tablecloth or plastic bag), and attach to the poster under the words "No Absorption" (or "Not Absorbed").

Use material that shows some absorption (e.g., piece of polyester or nylon), and attach to the poster under the words "Some Absorption" (or "Some Absorbed").

Use material that shows good absorption (e.g., piece of cotton or paper towel), and attach to the poster under the words "Full Absorption" (or "All Absorbed").

Materials

- wax paper
- plastic wrap
- construction paper
- materials of varying absorbency (e.g., paper towels, coffee filters, vinyl tablecloth, polyester, nylon)
- food colouring
- two index cards (Record "Solids" on one and "Liquids" on the other.)

14

- pictures of various solids and liquids (one picture for each student)
- edible liquids varying in transparency and viscosity (e.g., cooking oil, vinegar, milk, water, liquid chocolate, molasses, syrup)
- clear containers to hold liquids (Label containers A, B, C, and so on.)
- Template: Properties of Liquids (2.14.1)
- paper towels
- eyedroppers
- clear tape
- scissors
- containers of water (to rinse eyedroppers)
- newspaper (to cover work areas)
- chart paper
- markers
- writing paper
- hand sanitizer or hand-washing facilities
- forks (several for each student)
- stopwatch
- computer/tablet with internet access
- water
- milk
- syrup
- vegetable oil
- pocket chart*
- Learning-Centre Task Card: Does a Thick Liquid Travel Differently Than a Thin Liquid? (2.14.2)
- Learning-Centre Template: Racetrack (2.14.3)
- Learning-Centre Template: Does a Thick Liquid Travel Differently Than a Thin Liquid? (2.14.4) (optional)
- sturdy cardboard
- sticky notes
- concept web (from lesson 12)

*NOTE: If a pocket chart is not available, attach the index card labels to a sheet of chart paper, and use reusable adhesive putty to display pictures.

Engage

Provide each student with one picture of a solid or a liquid. Place the index cards labelled "Solids" and "Liquids" at opposite ends of the top row of the pocket chart. Have students look at their pictures. Ask:

- Is your picture an example of a solid or a liquid?

Have students place their pictures in the pocket chart under the correct heading. If they need support, they can reference the concept web (from lesson 12). When all pictures are displayed, have students focus on the solids. Ask:

- Do any of the pictures need to be moved?
- How do you know all these items are solids?
- What are the properties of solids?

Next, have students focus on the liquids. Ask:

- Do any of the pictures need to be moved?
- What makes all the items in these pictures liquids?

Remove all pictures of solids from the pocket chart, leaving just liquids on display.

Introduce the guided inquiry question: **What are some properties of liquids?**

Explore Part One

 SAFETY NOTE: Ensure all materials used in the classroom are nontoxic, and always be aware of any student allergies. Before beginning this activity, have students wash their hands or use hand sanitizer. Remind them that proper sanitation is a very important part of good health. Also, remind students that, when using their sense of taste to observe a substance, as in the following task, there is a proper and sanitary way to do so: each student may dip a fork into the substance once, and taste it off the end of their fork. Double-dipping is not allowed. Using forks will prevent students from ingesting too much of any liquid.

14

Organize the class into working groups, and provide each group with newspaper and a labelled container of liquid. Challenge students to infer the identity of the liquid in their container. Stress that no liquid is to be tasted without your permission; in this case, the liquids may be tasted, since they are all safe for human consumption. Ensure all students are familiar with the proper and sanitary way to taste a substance using a fork.

Remind students they may also observe, smell, and touch the liquids, and move the containers to see how the liquids move.

SAFETY NOTE: Teach students to smell items by waving a hand across the container toward their noses (wafting), instead of directly inhaling over the open container.

Give students plenty of time to observe and discuss their liquid; encourage them to come to a group consensus about its identity.

On chart paper, make a recording sheet as in the following Template: Properties of Liquids (2.14.1):

Download this template at <www.portageandmainpress.com/product/HOSMatterK2>.

Use this template as a guide for small group investigation or for students to construct their own data recording sheets. Complete this chart as a class during or following this investigation.

With students still in their groups, approach the group with container A, and ask:

- How would you describe this liquid?
- What liquid do you think is in container A?

Repeat this questioning with each group and for each liquid, and come to a class consensus about the properties and identity of each liquid.

Focus on the transparency of the liquids. Ask:

- How do the liquids all look different from each other?
- Which liquids are clear (or transparent)?

Using the liquids as examples, introduce the terms *transparent* (clear), *translucent* (not clear, but light can pass through), and *opaque* (light cannot pass through).

Have groups classify their liquid as transparent, translucent, or opaque. Encourage students to use these terms as they discuss each liquid's classification.

Introduce *viscosity* (the flow or thickness of liquids) by having students gently move the containers back and forth to see how quickly the liquids flow. Have students use descriptive words to describe viscosity (e.g., *thick, thin, runny, oozing*). Students can pour some of the liquid onto newspaper to test viscosity, and then, as a class, order the liquids according to viscosity.

To introduce the term *absorbency*, provide each group with an eyedropper and paper towels. Have groups place a few drops of their liquid on

Properties of Matter for Grades K–2

the paper towel and observe how the liquid is absorbed (not absorbed at all, some absorbed, all absorbed). Students can then order the liquids according to absorbency.

Explore Part Two

Focus on the properties of maple sap and maple syrup, and how viscosity plays a role in the production of maple syrup. Read stories such as:

- *Maple Moon* by Connie Brummel Crook
- *The Maple Syrup Book* by Marilyn Linton
- *At Grandpa's Sugar Bush* by Margaret Carney

Next, show the following videos:

- "Kleekhoot Gold Bigleaf Maple Syrup" <https://www.youtube.com/watch?v=flaT5SoSSRg>
- "Sweet success: B.C. First Nation launches commercial maple syrup venture" <https://vancouverisland.ctvnews.ca/sweet-success-b-c-first-nation-launches-commercial-maple-syrup-venture-1.3318912>
- "Tapping Into The Science Of The Maple Sugar Harvest" <https://www.youtube.com/watch?v=oxPaD_2K_08>
- "How to Make Maple Syrup" <https://www.youtube.com/watch?v=7SrdKlzvHSs>

Review the videos and discuss the process for tapping the sap and making maple sugar and syrup. Using the videos for reference, discuss how the thickness of maple syrup and maple sap are related. Students can also observe the role of the Sun and the role of heat. They will see how heat can be used to both thicken maple sap and thin maple syrup.

As an extension to this activity, invite a local Elder, Knowledge Keeper, or maple syrup producer to speak to the class about how maple syrup is made and used in British Columbia.

NOTE: See Indigenous Perspectives and Knowledge, page 9, for guidelines for inviting Elders and Knowledge Keepers to speak to students.

Expand

Provide students with an opportunity to explore properties of liquids further by posing their own inquiry questions for personalized learning. They may wish to:

- Initiate a project at the Makerspace centre, such as designing and constructing a container that can hold a liquid.
- Explore Loose Parts related to properties of liquids. For example, as a class, collect various small objects used with liquids (e.g., spoons, ladles, basters, measuring cups and spoons, syringes, small spray bottles). Students can explore the Loose Parts to generate their own inquiry questions.
- Search the internet for images of clean water and polluted water. Explore similarities and differences in their properties as well as causes of water pollution.
- Explore the properties of liquids and their implications for everyday life. For example, investigate water in a local pond, stream, river, or lake. Is it transparent, translucent, or opaque?

 SAFETY NOTE: Ensure safety considerations around water and supervise such activities.

- Use eyedroppers, cookie sheets, and paper towels to test the absorbency of various liquids and record observations.
- Conduct an investigation or experiment based on their own inquiry questions.

NOTE: Ensure a water table is available to further explore liquids. Provide a variety of materials for play (e.g., eye droppers, spray bottles, funnels, water wheels, various containers).

14

As students explore and select ideas to expand learning, provide support and guidance as needed, and offer access to materials and resources that will enable students to conduct their chosen investigations.

Learning Centre

NOTE: Mount the Learning-Centre Template: Racetrack (2.14.3) onto cardboard to provide a sturdy racing surface to use at the learning centre. Also, demonstrate and have students practise using the stopwatch before starting this activity.

At the learning centre, provide containers of water, milk, syrup, and vegetable oil, as well as eyedroppers, wax paper, paper towels, clear tape, a stopwatch, and writing paper. Also provide a copy of the Learning-Centre Task Card: Does a Thick Liquid Travel Differently Than a Thin Liquid? (2.14.2) and several copies of the Learning-Centre Template: Racetrack (2.14.3).

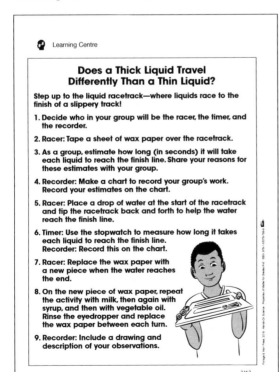

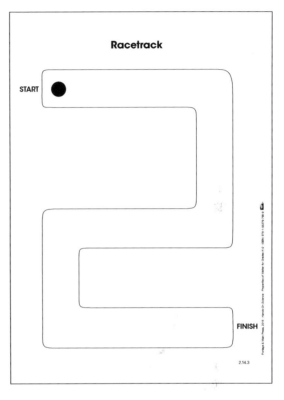

Download these templates at <www.portageandmainpress.com/product/HOSMatterK2>.

Students will test the viscosity of liquids on the racetrack. In groups, have students use tape to attach a sheet of wax paper over the racetrack. Stress the importance of keeping all other variables the same for each liquid they test on the racetrack (e.g., number of drops, drop location on the racetrack).

Challenge students to estimate how long it will take each liquid to reach the finish line, discuss why they made those estimates (rationale), and then use the stopwatch to measure. Have students design their own data recording sheet, or provide copies of the Learning-Centre Template: Does a Thick Liquid Travel Differently Than a Thin Liquid? (2.14.4):

▶

14

Does a Thick Liquid Travel Differently Than a Thin Liquid?

Liquid	Estimate: How long will it take the drop to reach the finish line?	Result: How long did it actually take the drop to reach the finish line?
water		
syrup		
milk		
vegetable oil		

2.14.4

Have each group decide who will be the racer, the timer, and the recorder. Begin by having the racer place a drop of water at the starting point. When the timer starts the stopwatch, have the racer tip the racetrack back and forth to get the liquid to move along the track. When the liquid has reached the finish line, have the recorder note the actual time it took. Have the group replace the wax paper and repeat the activity with the milk, the syrup, and the vegetable oil, rinsing the eyedropper and replacing the wax paper between each test. Ensure each student has an opportunity to be the racer, the timer, and the recorder.

Embed Part One: Talking Circle

Revisit the guided inquiry question: **What are some properties of liquids?** Have students share their knowledge and experiences, provide examples, and ask further inquiry questions.

Embed Part Two

- Add to the concept web as students learn new concepts, answer some of their own inquiry questions, and ask new inquiry questions.

- Add new terms and illustrations to the word wall. Include the words in languages other than English, such as Indigenous languages, as appropriate.

- Focus on students' use of the Core Competencies. Have students reflect on how they used one of the Core Competencies (Thinking, Communicating, or Personal and Social Skills) during the various lesson activities. Project one of the CORE COMPETENCY DISCUSSION PROMPTS templates (pages 38–42), and use it to inspire group reflection. Referring to the template, choose one or two "I Can" statements on which to focus. Students then use the "I Can" statements to provide evidence of how they demonstrated that competency. Ask questions directly related to that competency to inspire discussion. For example:
  - How did you show how you can work in a group today? (Communication)

  Have students reflect orally, encouraging participation, questions, and the sharing of evidence (see page 29 for more information on these templates).

  As part of this process, students can also set goals. For example, ask:
  - What would you do differently next time and why?
  - How will you know if you are successful in meeting your goal?

- To encourage self-reflection, provide prompts that students can use to cite examples of how they have used the Core Competencies in their learning. For this purpose, the CORE COMPETENCY SELF-REFLECTION FRAMES

14

(pages 44–47) can be used throughout the learning process. There are five frames provided to address the Core Competencies: Communication, Creative Thinking, Critical Thinking, Positive Personal and Cultural Identity, and Personal Awareness and Responsibility. Conference individually with students to support self-reflection, or students may complete prompts using words and pictures.

Again, have students set goals by considering what they might do differently on future tasks and how they will know if they are successful in meeting their goal.

NOTE: Use the same prompts from these templates over time to see how thinking changes with different activities.

Enhance

- **Family Connection**: Provide students with the following sentence starter:
    - Some properties of liquids in our home are _____.

    Have students complete the sentence starter at home. Family members can help the student draw and write about this topic. Have students share their sentences with the class.

- Discuss properties of liquids that affect everyday activities and uses. For example, ask:
    - When you swim in water, is it thick or thin (viscosity)?
    - How would swimming be different if the water was like syrup?
    - How would canoeing or kayaking be affected if water was thick like syrup?
- Access the interactive activity, Properties of Liquids, from the Unit 3 folder in the ***Hands-On Science and Technology, Grade 2*** download. While these interactive activities were originally developed for the Ontario curriculum, they present valuable learning opportunities across grades and provincial curriculums. Find this download at: <https://www.portageandmainpress.com/product/hands-on-interactive-for-science-and-technology-grade-2/>.

15 Can Liquids and Solids Be Mixed Together?

Information for Teachers

The term *solubility* describes the degree to which a solid, liquid, or gas can dissolve into another solid, liquid, or gas. The term *dissolve*, or *dissolution*, means the particles of a solid (the *solute*) spread out equally into a liquid (the *solvent*). Stirring spreads out the solute particles in the solvent, increasing the chance that they will come into contact with solvent molecules. Heating makes the particles move faster and the rate of dissolving increases.

Materials

- food colouring (including red)
- clear glass of water
- chart paper
- markers
- small transparent jars or containers with lids (e.g., food storage containers, baby food jars) (one for each working group)
- various liquids (e.g., baby oil, milk, juice)
- stopwatch or timer (optional)
- jugs of water (one for each working group)
- vegetable oil
- honey
- syrup
- dish soap
- tall, clear glass tumblers
- funnels
- coffee filters (or paper towels)
- newspaper (to cover work areas)
- computer/tablet with internet access (optional)
- spoons
- small, lightweight items (e.g., thumbtacks, paper clips, safety pins, small buttons)
- paper (scrap or writing)
- digital cameras (one for each working group)
- clear glasses (three for each working group)
- granulated white sugar
- 15-mL measuring spoons (one for each working group)
- 5-mL measuring spoons
- drawing paper
- craft sticks or pencils
- shallow transparent trays (e.g., petri or baking dish) (two for each working group)
- 50-mL measuring cups or graduated cylinders
- "lab coats" (e.g., repurposed adult-size white shirts)
- Learning-Centre Task Card: What More Can We Learn About Liquids? (2.15.1)
- sticky notes
- concept web (from lesson 12)

Engage

Display food colouring and a clear glass of water. Have students describe each liquid, and then predict what they think will happen if the food colouring is added to the water.

Test their predictions by adding a few drops of food colouring to the water. Have them observe carefully as the liquids mix. Do not stir, but allow the food colouring to spread through the water. Ask:

- What can we do to mix the two liquids better?

Now, stir the mixture with a spoon. Ask:

- How is this liquid different from the two liquids with which we started?
- Will the liquids separate again, or will they stay mixed?

Have students share their ideas and predictions. Ask:

- What other liquids have you seen mixed together?

Students will likely have had many experiences mixing liquids for different reasons and on

15

different occasions (e.g., mixing dish soap with water, making a bubble bath with water and bath suds, mixing chocolate syrup into milk, mixing oil and vinegar for salad dressing). Have students think of two liquids they have mixed or have seen someone in their family mix. Encourage them to describe how each liquid looks, and describe what is done to combine the mixture (e.g., parts mixed hot, cold, with a blender, with a spoon). Then, ask them to describe what the mixture looks like after mixing.

Introduce the guided inquiry question: **Can liquids and solids be mixed together?**

Explore Part One

Focus on the lesson's inquiry question. Model some wonderings students might have about the question. For example:

- I wonder what happens if dish soap is mixed with salt.
- I wonder if sugar and syrup mix together easily.

Encourage students to make predictions based on wonderings. Have students share their own wonderings and record these along with their predictions on chart paper.

Organize the class into working groups, and provide each group with small transparent containers or jars with lids (e.g., food storage containers, baby food jars), water, vegetable oil, other liquids (e.g., baby oil, juice, milk), a 15-mL measuring spoon, food colouring, and a digital camera.

Encourage students to photograph the inquiry process.

Have students measure 30 mL of water and pour it into a small container. Ask:

- If you add some oil to the container, what do you think will happen?

- Will the two liquids mix together?

Have students measure 30 mL of vegetable oil and slowly add it to the water in the container. Ask:

- Do the two liquids mix together?

Now, tell students to put lids tightly on the containers and shake them. Ask:

- What happened?
- What do you think will happen if you leave the container sitting on the table for a few minutes?

Have students wait three minutes, encouraging them to help measure the time.

NOTE: Model for students how to watch the second hand of the classroom clock. Students can watch for it to go around three times. Alternatively, students can use a stopwatch or timer. Many visual timers are available online, such as <https://www.online-stopwatch.com>.

When three minutes have passed, ask:

- Did the liquids stay mixed together?

Next, have students add two drops of food colouring to their liquid mixtures. Ask:

- Look at the side of your container. What do you see happening?

Have students use a pencil or craft stick to gently push down the food colouring to the water level. Ask:

- What happens now?

Provide students with scrap or writing paper. Encourage them to record their investigation and observations. This may be done through diagrams and/or words.

Have students select, test, and record observations about mixing other liquids (e.g., baby oil, juice, milk) with water.

Allow plenty of time for students to experiment with measuring and mixing liquids. Challenge students to predict, and then test, what happens when two or more liquids are mixed together with water.

Use a digital camera to photograph the experiment. These photographs can be used to create a class book to record the experiment, or put in a learning centre for students to write about or continue to explore.

Explore Part Two

Organize the class into working groups, and provide each group with a jug of water, a clear glass, 5-mL measuring spoon, a small container of sugar, and spoons. Spread out newspaper at each group's work station.

Have students fill their glass half full with water. Ask:

- What will happen if you add sugar to the cup of water?
- Will it make any difference if you stir the water after the sugar has been added?

Have students measure 5 mL of sugar into the cup, and observe without stirring. Then, tell them to stir the water and observe the sugar. Ask:

- Is the sugar a solid or a liquid?
- Is the water a solid or a liquid?
- Has the sugar disappeared?
- Do you think there is any sugar in the water?
- What do you think has happened?

Have students use spoons to taste the water (dipping only once!) to observe the presence of sugar. Introduce the term *dissolve*. Stress that the solid is not disappearing. The solid is breaking down into small parts throughout a liquid. Although the sugar cannot be seen, it is still present in the solution.

Have students measure and mix a second solution of sugar and water identical in proportions to the first. Provide groups with funnels and coffee filters (or paper towels). Have them construct a filter system by placing the coffee filter or paper towel into the funnel. Ask:

- What do you think will happen when you pour the sugar water through the funnel?
- Will there still be sugar in the water after it has been filtered?
- Will the filter catch any of the sugar?
- Do you have any questions about this investigation?

Record students' inquiry questions, and address them during the investigation.

Have students test their predictions by pouring the sugar water through the filter into another clear glass that has been labelled "Filtered." Ask students to examine both the filter and the filtered solution. Ask:

- Do you see any sugar on the filter? (No)
- Does the filtered sugar water look any different from the sugar water in the first glass? (No)

Have students again use clean spoons to taste both the filtered solution and the unfiltered solution, and compare the two.

Then have them label two shallow trays "Filtered" and "Unfiltered." Ask students to pour the solutions into the appropriate trays. Ask:

- What will happen if these solutions are left uncovered for a few days?

Leave the trays in a warm area, and observe and compare the residues as the water evaporates. Have students use a digital camera to photograph the results of this investigation.

15

Expand

Provide students with an opportunity to explore properties of liquids further by posing their own inquiry questions for personalized learning. They may wish to:

- Initiate a project at the Makerspace centre, such as designing and constructing a device that helps dissolve sugar in water.
- Explore Loose Parts related to recycling with collections of various granular products (e.g., sugar, salt, baking powder, sand, beads, coffee) stored in zipper-lock bags. Students can explore the Loose Parts to generate their own inquiry questions.
- Test other liquids for solubility.
- Test various liquids for their ability to dissolve sugar.
- Test different solids for their ability to dissolve in water (e.g., sand, drink mix, salt, flour).
- Conduct an investigation or experiment based on their own inquiry questions.

NOTE: Ensure a water table is available to further explore liquids. Provide a variety of materials for play (e.g., eyedroppers, spray bottles, funnels, water wheels, various containers, objects for floating and sinking).

As students explore and select ideas to expand learning, provide support and guidance as needed, and offer access to materials and resources that will enable students to conduct their chosen investigations.

Learning Centre

At the learning centre, provide "lab coats" (e.g., repurposed adult-size white shirts), red food colouring, honey, syrup, 50-mL measuring cup(s) or graduated cylinders, dish soap, water, vegetable oil, clear glass tumblers, spoons, drawing paper, and small, lightweight items (e.g., thumbtacks, paper clips, safety pins, small buttons) along with a copy of the Learning-

Centre Task Card: What More Can We Learn About Liquids? (2.15.1):

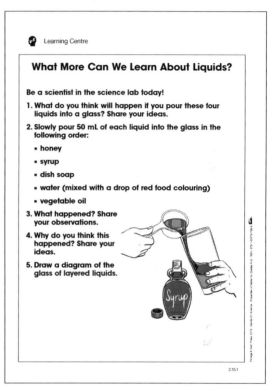

Download this template at <www.portageandmainpress.com/product/HOSMatterK2>.

Have students create interesting table centrepieces by layering liquids in a density column. Have students slowly pour 50 mL of each liquid into a tumbler in the following order:

1. honey (bottom)
2. syrup
3. dish soap
4. water (mixed with a drop of red food colouring)
5. vegetable oil (top)

Encourage students to pour each liquid onto a spoon first, then gently tip the tumbler on a slight angle and pour the liquid down the side of the

▶

Properties of Matter for Grades K–2 145

tumbler. This will help prevent the liquids from splashing and mixing together.

Have students theorize about what is happening and why.

NOTE: The densest (heaviest) layer is on the bottom and the least dense (lightest) layer is on the top.

Finally, have students suspend small, lightweight items in the column (e.g., thumbtacks, paper clips, safety pins, small buttons). Have them first predict, and then test to determine, whether various items float or sink in the liquids.

Embed Part One: Talking Circle

Revisit the guided inquiry question: **Can liquids and solids be mixed together?** Have students share their knowledge and experiences, provide examples, and ask further inquiry questions.

Embed Part Two

- Add to the concept web as students learn new concepts, answer some of their own inquiry questions, and ask new inquiry questions.
- Add new terms and illustrations to the word wall. Include the words in languages other than English, such as Indigenous languages, as appropriate.
- Focus on students' use of the Core Competencies. Have students reflect on how they used one of the Core Competencies (Thinking, Communicating, or Personal and Social Skills) during the various lesson activities. Project one of the CORE COMPETENCY DISCUSSION PROMPTS templates (pages 38–42), and use it to inspire group reflection. Referring to the template, choose one or two "I Can" statements on which to focus. Students then use the "I Can" statements to provide evidence of how they demonstrated that competency. Ask questions directly related to that competency to inspire discussion. For example:
  - How did you work safely with materials today? (Personal Awareness and Responsibility)

Have students reflect orally, encouraging participation, questions, and the sharing of evidence (see page 29 for more information on these templates).

As part of this process, students can also set goals. For example, ask:
- What would you do differently next time and why?
- How will you know if you are successful in meeting your goal?

- To encourage self-reflection, provide prompts that students can use to cite examples of how they have used the Core Competencies in their learning. For this purpose, the CORE COMPETENCY SELF-REFLECTION FRAMES (pages 44–47) can be used throughout the learning process. There are five frames provided to address the Core Competencies: Communication, Creative Thinking, Critical Thinking, Positive Personal and Cultural Identity, and Personal Awareness and Responsibility. Conference individually with students to support self-reflection, or students may complete prompts using words and pictures.

Again, have students set goals by considering what they might do differently on future tasks, and how they will know if they are successful in meeting their goal.

NOTE: Use the same prompts from these templates over time to see how thinking changes with different activities.

15

Enhance

- **Family Connection**: Provide students with the following sentence starter:
    - Some solids and liquids in our home that we can safely mix together are _____.

    Have students complete the sentence starter at home. Family members can help the student draw and write about this topic. Have students share their sentences with the class.

    ⚠️ **SAFETY NOTE:** This activity should be fully supervised by adults. Ensure all solids and liquids used are safe for mixing together. Avoid using products with caution symbols (e.g., cleaning products). Use everyday solids and liquids (e.g., cooking or baking ingredients). Send a note home with students with the above guidelines to help ensure students conduct the experiment safely and with adult supervision.

- Access the interactive activity, Liquid Interactions, from the Unit 3 folder in the ***Hands-On Science and Technology, Grade 2*** download. While these interactive activities were originally developed for the Ontario curriculum, they present valuable learning opportunities across grades and provincial curriculums. Find this download at: <https://www.portageandmainpress.com/product/hands-on-interactive-for-science-and-technology-grade-2/>.

Properties of Matter for Grades K–2

16 | How Can We Combine Solids and Liquids to Make Useful Products?

Materials

- commercial Silly Putty*
- commercial paste*
- commercial soft modelling clay*
- Image Bank: First Peoples Clothing (see Appendix, page 175)
- commercial fabric dye*
- large metal pot
- square fabric swatches for dyeing (preferably white)
- craft sticks
- assortment of plants or plant parts for making dyes (e.g., berries; beets; red cabbage; parsley; olives; tree leaves; flowers; beans; tree bark; orange, lemon, and tangerine peels; carrots; coffee; purple grapes)
- potato mashers or forks
- newspaper
- chart paper
- markers
- kettle (teacher use only)
- knife (teacher use only)
- food colouring (optional)
- containers for dying fabric
- flour
- water
- measuring cups
- large mixing bowls
- heavy mixing spoons
- measuring spoons
- plastic containers with lids (e.g., yogurt or margarine containers)
- refrigerator access
- projection device (optional)
- scrap paper
- smocks and paint shirts
- white glue
- liquid starch
- bowls with tightly sealing lids (optional)
- plastic freezer bags (optional)
- salt
- alum
- vegetable oil
- sticky notes
- concept web (from lesson 12)

*NOTE: Provide commercial products where specified for the following activities. Students will be comparing commercial products with homemade products.

Engage

Organize the class into working groups, and provide each group with a sheet of chart paper, markers, and samples of commercial Silly Putty (or a similar product), commercial paste, and commercial modelling clay.

Ask students to divide their chart paper into three equal sections and title each section with the names of the three products. Have students observe, examine, and manipulate the products, recording the observable characteristics of each on their chart paper.

Have the groups share their observations. Ask:

- For what is each product used?
- What characteristics make it useful?
- What properties does Silly Putty need for it to be useful?
- What properties does paste need for it to be useful? Modelling clay?

Explain to students that many useful products can be made by mixing solids and liquids. They will now have an opportunity to make some of their own products by mixing solids and liquids, and to compare and evaluate them.

Introduce the guided inquiry question: **How can we combine solids and liquids to make useful products?**

16

Explore Part One

> **SAFETY NOTE:** The following recipe requires boiling water and should be conducted as a demonstration only. Students should not handle the boiling water.

As a demonstration, make some homemade soft modelling dough. Collect the following materials: 1250 mL flour, 250 mL salt, 60 mL alum, 30 mL vegetable oil, 750 mL water, a large bowl, kettle, heavy mixing spoon, and food colouring (optional).

Boil water. Add food colouring to the water (optional). Mix dry ingredients in a large mixing bowl. Stir in 750 mL of boiling water. When the mixture has cooled enough to handle, knead it on a table until the dough is thoroughly mixed. Keep the dough in a tightly covered container, and refrigerate overnight.

Distribute the homemade dough to students. Have students describe its observable characteristics. Then distribute some of the commercially made dough to students, and have them compare it with the homemade dough, testing each product to determine its effectiveness for modelling (e.g., easy to manipulate, holds its shape).

Explore Part Two

Organize the class into working groups, and provide each group with the ingredients and supplies necessary to make paste: flour, water, measuring cups, large mixing bowl, and mixing spoon. Ask:

- Which ingredients are solids?
- Which ingredients are liquids?

Give students the following directions:

- Pour 250 mL of flour into the bowl, and mix with 325 mL of water.
- Stir until smooth. The paste should be creamy; add flour if the paste is too thin, or water if it becomes too thick.

NOTE: The paste can be stored in sealed containers (such as recycled margarine or yogurt containers) and used for classroom crafts and activities.

When students have completed the paste, have them describe its observable characteristics. Distribute some of the commercial paste to each group along with some scrap paper, and ask students to compare the homemade paste to the commercial paste, using scrap paper to test each product to determine its effectiveness as an adhesive.

Explore Part Three

Now, provide each group with the ingredients and supplies necessary to make Silly Putty: 150 mL white glue, 75 mL liquid starch, a bowl with tightly sealing lid or plastic freezer bag, and a heavy mixing spoon. Ask:

- Which ingredients are solids?
- Which ingredients are liquids?

Give students the following directions:

Pour both ingredients into the bowl. Mix them together using a heavy mixing spoon. Pour off the leftover liquid. Store the putty overnight in a tightly covered container or a plastic bag. In the morning, knead the putty to soften it.

When the Silly Putty is complete, have students describe its observable characteristics. Distribute some of the commercial Silly Putty to students, and have them compare it to the homemade product. Test each putty product to determine its effectiveness as a modelling material (e.g., easy to manipulate, holds its shape).

Explore Part Four

Have students look at their clothing and the clothing of their peers, paying special attention to the colours in the clothing. Ask:

- How do you think the different colours are created on fabrics?
- Where do you think dyes come from?

Create a tally of the colours in students' clothing—tops and bottoms. For example:

Colour	Top	Bottom
Red		
Blue		
Green		
Grey		
Multi-colour		

Use the tally chart to read and interpret data, then have students pose questions about the information presented in it. For example:

- Which colour do we see the most in our tops?
- Which colour do we see the least in our bottoms?
- In total, how many clothing pieces are brown?

Have other students in the class respond to these questions.

Extend the activity by having students create a pictograph using small paper cut-outs of shirts or pants.

Explore Part Five

Invite a local Elder or Knowledge Keeper to share and discuss creating natural dyes for clothing and art.

NOTE: See Indigenous Perspectives and Knowledge, page 9, for guidelines for inviting Elders and Knowledge Keepers to speak to students.

Display the Image Bank: First Peoples Clothing. Have students examine and discuss the clothing, focusing on colours. Ask:

- How do you think First Peoples dye clothing?
- What natural materials might they use?
- Have you ever used a plant in such a way that it left a stain on you? (e.g., sliding on the grass, spilling blueberries on clothing, cutting up beets, rubbing a buttercup flower)

Have students share their experiences.

Explore Part Six

NOTE: The following activity can be done as a whole-class experiment or at an activity centre with an adult supervisor.

Demonstrate the process for dying fabric. Follow instructions provided with commercial fabric dye. After the demonstration, when the fabric is dyed, ask:

- Of what do you think fabric dye is made?

Have students share their inferences.

Have students put on smocks or paint shirts, and, as a class, select one plant (see Materials) to use for dyeing. Organize the class into small working groups, and distribute to each group some of the plant, a potato masher or fork, and a bowl or container in which to mash the plant. Have students mash their portion of the plant.

NOTE: If students are not able to mash the plant, have an adult cut it up, or leave it whole.

Distribute measuring cups, and tell students to measure 125 mL of the mashed plant. Combine all portions of the mashed plant into a large metal pot, and add 500 mL of water. Boil the mixture for about five minutes, or until the water becomes coloured. Some plants may take longer, while others may require more water.

16

> ⚠ **SAFETY NOTE:** For the safety of all students, boiling must be done by an adult only, away from student access.

When the water is coloured, remove the pot from the heat source, and let it cool.

Now, distribute to each working group a container for dyeing and a square swatch of white fabric, and have students place the fabric into the empty container. Have the groups pour some of the cooled, coloured water into their containers. Distribute craft sticks, and tell students to use them to help ensure the fabric is completely covered with coloured water.

Have students predict the colour of the fabric after it has soaked in the dye overnight.

Leave the fabric pieces in the containers overnight. The next day, have students remove their fabric piece from the dye, and lay it flat on newspaper to dry.

Repeat the dyeing process with different plants to compare how various plants produce colour on the material.

Expand

Provide students with an opportunity to explore how solids and liquids can be combined to make useful products further by posing their own inquiry questions for personalized learning. They may wish to:

- Initiate a project at the Makerspace centre, such as creating a puppet play to demonstrate the properties of solids and liquids.
- Explore Loose Parts related to solids and liquids with collections of various samples of modelling materials (e.g., homemade and commercial Silly Putty, play dough, modelling clay). Store samples in zipper-lock bags. Students can explore the Loose Parts to generate their own inquiry questions.
- Research or create their own recipes for play dough, paste, or other products (see Inquiry Through Research, page 26).
- Explore Indigenous art and techniques to create colour.
- Conduct an investigation or experiment based on their own inquiry questions.

As students explore and select ideas to expand learning, provide support and guidance as needed, and offer access to materials and resources that will enable students to conduct their chosen investigations.

Embed Part One: Talking Circle

Revisit the guided inquiry question: **How can we combine solids and liquids to make useful products?** Have students share their knowledge and experiences, provide examples, and ask further inquiry questions.

Embed Part Two

- Add to the concept web as students learn new concepts, answer some of their own inquiry questions, and ask new inquiry questions.
- Add new terms and illustrations to the word wall. Include the words in languages other than English, such as Indigenous languages, as appropriate.
- Focus on students' use of the Core Competencies. Have students reflect on how they used one of the Core Competencies (Thinking, Communicating, or Personal and Social Skills) during the various lesson activities. Project one of the CORE COMPETENCY DISCUSSION PROMPTS templates (pages 38–42), and use it to inspire group reflection. Referring to the template, choose one or two "I Can" statements on which to focus. Students then use the "I Can" statements to provide evidence of how they demonstrated that competency. Ask

▶

questions directly related to that competency to inspire discussion. For example:

- How did you decide which questions to ask today? (Critical Thinking)

Have students reflect orally, encouraging participation, questions, and the sharing of evidence (see page 29 for more information on these templates).

As part of this process, students can also set goals. For example, ask:

- What would you do differently next time and why?
- How will you know if you are successful in meeting your goal?

■ To encourage self-reflection, provide prompts that students can use to cite examples of how they have used the Core Competencies in their learning. For this purpose, the CORE COMPETENCY SELF-REFLECTION FRAMES (pages 44–47) can be used throughout the learning process. There are five frames provided to address the Core Competencies: Communication, Creative Thinking, Critical Thinking, Positive Personal and Cultural Identity, and Personal Awareness and Responsibility. Conference individually with students to support self-reflection, or students may complete prompts using words and pictures.

Again, have students set goals by considering what they might do differently on future tasks and how they will know if they are successful in meeting their goal.

NOTE: Use the same prompts from these templates over time to see how thinking changes with different activities.

Enhance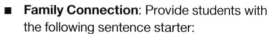

- **Family Connection:** Provide students with the following sentence starter:
    - We can make a useful product at home by combining solids and liquids, such as _____.

    Have students complete the sentence starter at home. Family members can help the student draw and write about this topic. Have students share their sentences with the class.

- Read *Pete the Cat: I Love My White Shoes* by Eric Litwin.

- Further explore the use of natural dyes using the following links:
    - "Materials: Traditional Dyes" <https://umistapotlatch.ca/enseignants-education/cours_9-lesson_9-eng.php>
    - "Soils, Plants, and First Nations" <https://scientistinresidence.ca/science-lesson-plans/soils-plants-and-first-nations/>

- Explore the history of Silly Putty by reviewing with students the article "The History of Silly Putty" <https://www.thoughtco.com/the-history-of-silly-putty-1779330>.

- Access the interactive activity Liquid Interactions, from the Unit 3 folder in the *Hands-On Science and Technology, Grade 2* download. While these interactive activities were originally developed for the Ontario curriculum, they present valuable learning opportunities across grades and provincial curriculums. Find this download at: <https://www.portageandmainpress.com/product/hands-on-interactive-for-science-and-technology-grade-2/>.

17 What Are the Properties of Air?

Information for Teachers

A *gas* occupies the space not taken up by solids and liquids and is a state of matter. Gases are made up of molecules that vibrate quickly and collide off of each other. These molecules can move very far apart from each other. A gas does not have a definite shape or a definite volume.

Air is a mixture of gases: oxygen (approximately 20%), nitrogen (approximately 78%), and small amounts of water vapour, carbon dioxide, and argon.

Materials

- uninflated balloons
- permanent markers in several colours
- basins of water (or a water table)
- clear cups (one for each working group)
- paper towels
- Learning-Centre Task Card: How Does a Balloon Rocket Show Us the Properties of Air? (2.17.1)
- scissors
- cardboard
- 6-cm diameter cardboard tracers
- ruler
- map of local area
- map of traditional territories of First Peoples in British Columbia (see lesson 1)
- drawing paper
- tissue paper (cut into long, thin strips)
- glue
- hole punches
- chart papers
- markers
- thin paint
- art paper
- drinking straws
- shopping bags (optional)
- digital camera (optional)
- kite (optional)
- concept web (from lesson 12)
- herringbone chart (lesson 3)

Engage

Review the herringbone chart (lesson 3) and concept web (lesson 12). Ask:

- What have we learned about objects and materials?
- Of which different materials can objects be made?
- What is an example of a solid?
- What is an example of a liquid?
- Is air a solid?
- Is air a liquid?
- What is air?

Discuss students' background knowledge of air and gases.

Have all students observe one another while taking a deep breath. Ask:

- When taking deep breaths, what do you notice about your chest?
- Why do you think your chest expands, or gets bigger, when you take a breath?

Discuss the fact that everyone breathes air, and when we take deep breaths, air enters our lungs.

Now, have students blow up balloons and observe what happens. Compare the inflated balloons with balloons that have not been inflated. Ask:

- Why did the balloons get bigger?
- What is inside the balloons?

Have students let the air out of their balloons and feel it "whooshing" by as it escapes. Stress the fact that even though air cannot be seen, it still takes up space. Have students observe air further by placing the balloons under water in a basin or water table while letting the air out. Bubbles prove that air is inside the balloon.

17

Introduce the guided inquiry question: **What are the properties of air?**

Explore Part One

Organize the class into working groups and provide each group with a basin of water, a clear cup, and a piece of paper towel. Ask:

- Which of these objects are solids?
- Which are liquids?
- Are there gases here as well?
- What is an example of a gas?

Have students crumple up the paper towel and place it inside the cup. Ask:

- What do you think will happen if you turn the cup upside down and put it in the basin of water?

Have students share their predictions. Then have them test their predictions by immersing the cup in the water. Ask:

- What happens to the paper towel?
- Why do you think the paper towel did not get wet?

Discuss the presence of air in the cup, even though it cannot be seen. The air in the cup stops the paper towel from getting wet because, as the cup is lowered into the water, the air presses against the water, taking up space.

Have students predict what will happen if the cup is turned upside down, immersed, and then slowly turned right side up. Test their predictions. Ask:

- What escapes from the cup?
- From where did this air come?
- Is the paper towel wet or dry?

Have students share their observations. Distribute drawing paper and have students draw labelled diagrams of this investigation.

Brainstorm evidence that demonstrates air exists, and have students provide statements. Record these on chart paper.

For example:

- We feel the air from a fan.
- I watch a tree sway on a windy day.
- I can blow out the flame of a candle.
- I can fly a kite in the air.
- I can whistle with air.

Explore Part Two

Provide students with thin paint, art paper, and drinking straws. Have each student place a small drop of paint on paper. Then have students blow through their straws toward the drops of paint, spreading the paint across the paper in various directions. Using a variety of colours will allow students to observe colour mixing. Have students use scissors to cut the paper into a long, thin sheet and create a top and bottom black border to make a wall hanging.

Explore Part Three

Take the class outdoors to the school playground, to a local park, or to a nature area.

Before the walk, be sure to review with students the importance of being respectful of nature. Review the anchor chart created in lesson 1.

As with all place-based learning activities:

- Identify the importance of place. Use a map of the local area to identify where the location is in relation to the school.
- Identify on whose traditional territory the school is located, as well as the traditional territory of the location for the nature walk, if different.
- Incorporate land acknowledgment using local protocols.

17

While outdoors, challenge students to explore air in nature. Try the following activities:

- determine the direction of the wind
- use a shopping bag to "capture" air
- take photographs that show objects being moved by wind or air
- fly a kite

Expand

Provide students with an opportunity to explore properties of air further by posing their own inquiry questions for personalized learning. They may wish to:

- Initiate a project at the Makerspace centre, such as designing and constructing a device that flies through the air using wind power.
- Explore Loose Parts related to air, such as collections of feathers, balloons, and straws. Students can explore the Loose Parts to generate their own inquiry questions.
- Use the Learning-Centre Template: Racetrack (2.14.3) from lesson 14 to set up races. Blow through a straw to move a variety of objects (e.g., cotton balls, pom poms, small balls, seeds) around the track.
- Conduct an investigation or experiment based on their own inquiry questions.

As students explore and select ideas to expand learning, provide support and guidance as needed, and offer access to materials and resources that will enable students to conduct their chosen investigations.

Learning Centre

At the learning centre, provide 6-cm diameter cardboard tracers; scissors; balloons; cardboard; tissue paper cut into long, thin strips (about the size of a straw); glue; and hole punches. Also provide a copy of the Learning-Centre Task Card: How Does a Balloon Rocket Show Us the Properties of Air? (2.17.1):

Learning Centre

How Does a Balloon Rocket Show Us the Properties of Air?

1. Use the circle tracer to trace a circle onto cardboard.
2. Cut out the circle.
3. Glue one end of the long, thin strips of tissue paper around the edge of the circle.
4. Punch a hole in the centre of the circle, and stick the end of a balloon through the hole.
5. Blow up the balloon and release it.
6. The balloon rocket will fly through the air.
7. Observe the direction the balloon moves.
8. Design a new rocket to see if it will travel farther than your first rocket.
9. Draw a diagram of your new rocket design.
10. Construct your rocket.
11. Compare your rocket to the rockets your friends have made. Which rocket travels the farthest? What part of its design helps it to travel the farthest?
12. Share your ideas and observations.

Download this template at <www.portageandmainpress.com/product/HOSMatterK2>.

Have students cut a circle from cardboard 6 cm in diameter, then glue one end of the long, thin strips of tissue paper around the edge of the circle. Students then punch a hole in the centre of the circle, and stick the end of a balloon through the hole. Blow up the balloon and release it. The balloon rocket will fly through the air. Students will see how air can make objects move. They will also observe that the direction the balloon moves depends on the direction of the escaping air. If air is escaping to the floor, the balloon will travel to the ceiling.

Embed Part One: Talking Circle

Revisit the guided inquiry question: **What are the properties of air?** Have students share their knowledge and experiences, provide examples, and ask further inquiry questions.

Embed Part Two

- Add to the concept web as students learn new concepts, answer some of their own inquiry questions, and ask new inquiry questions.
- Add new terms and illustrations to the word wall. Include the words in languages other than English, such as Indigenous languages, as appropriate.
- Focus on students' use of the Core Competencies. Have students reflect on how they used one of the Core Competencies (Thinking, Communicating, or Personal and Social Skills) during the various lesson activities. Project one of the CORE COMPETENCY DISCUSSION PROMPTS templates (pages 38–42), and use it to inspire group reflection. Referring to the template, choose one or two "I Can" statements on which to focus. Students then use the "I Can" statements to provide evidence of how they demonstrated that competency. Ask questions directly related to that competency to inspire discussion. For example:
    - What are you proud of in your learning today? (Personal Awareness and Responsibility)

Have students reflect orally, encouraging participation, questions, and the sharing of evidence (see page 29 for more information on these templates).

As part of this process, students can also set goals. For example, ask:

- What would you do differently next time and why?
- How will you know if you are successful in meeting your goal?
- To encourage self-reflection, provide prompts that students can use to cite examples of how they have used the Core Competencies in their learning. For this purpose, the CORE COMPETENCY SELF-REFLECTION FRAMES (pages 44–47) can be used throughout the learning process. There are five frames provided to address the Core Competencies: Communication, Creative Thinking, Critical Thinking, Positive Personal and Cultural Identity, and Personal Awareness and Responsibility. Conference individually with students to support self-reflection, or students may complete prompts using words and pictures.

Again, have students set goals by considering what they might do differently on future tasks and how they will know if they are successful in meeting their goal.

NOTE: Use the same prompts from these templates over time to see how thinking changes with different activities.

Enhance

- **Family Connection**: Provide students with the following sentence starter:
    - We know there is air in our home because _____.

    Have students complete the sentence starter at home. Family members can help the student draw and write about this topic. Have students share their sentences with the class.
- Watch an online video to explore how air takes up space:
    - "Air Occupies Space—Elementary Science" <https://www.youtube.com/watch?v=H3PxZfJPrpE>

17

- Watch an online video about how air contains oxygen:
  - "Air contains oxygen experiment - Elementary Science" <https://www.youtube.com/watch?v=xh1-YnI6Z_Q>
- Fill a glass with water. Wet a small cardboard coaster. Place the cardboard coaster on top of the glass. Hold the coaster in place and invert the glass over a basin or water table. When the water settles inside the glass, ask students what they think will happen when you remove your hand. Remove your hand from the coaster. The coaster should remain in place, with the water still inside the glass. Ask:
  - Where is the water and where is the air?
  - Is water heavier than air?
  - Why is there air above and below the water?

Gently shake the glass over a basin. Ask:
  - Why did the water stay in the glass?

Now, pull the coaster away from the glass. The water will rush out because the air can now enter the glass. As the air rises into the glass the water will fall out. The cardboard stayed in place because the outside air pressure on the cardboard was greater than the water pressure.

NOTE: By introducing air pressure, you may need to help students with the visual of air pushing up on the cardboard and water pushing down.

- Using straws and Ping-Pong balls, have students take part in a relay race by blowing the Ping-Pong balls across the room.
- Demonstrate the existence of oxygen in air, using a candle in a holder, matches, and a glass container.

SAFETY NOTE: Open flames are not permitted in most schools, so this activity may need to be done outdoors. For safety purposes, ensure that water is on hand. Stress that students should not do this experiment.

Light the candle and have students observe the flame. Cover the candle with the glass container. Have students share their observations (the flame will extinguish). Do this several times so students have an opportunity to observe, discuss, and make inferences as to why the flame goes out. (Fire requires oxygen. When the container is placed over the candle, the oxygen inside the container gets used up and the flame goes out.)

Properties of Matter for Grades K–2

18 | What Is a Physical Change?

Information for Teachers

All substances, whether the iron in a coat hanger or the cotton in a shirt, can undergo a *physical change*. This means the substance keeps its original properties (atoms and molecules) but may change its shape, volume, and/or temperature. A coat hanger can be bent, melted, or frozen, and it will still be made of iron. Similarly, if you remove a cotton shirt from a hanger and fold it to pack into a suitcase, you have temporarily altered the form of the shirt, but the substance and its properties remain the same.

Materials

- uninflated balloons
- chart paper
- markers
- scrap paper
- writing paper
- paper clips (large)
- elastic bands
- computer/tablet with internet access
- digital cameras
- student dictionaries
- modelling clay, Plasticine, or play dough (various colours)
- beads (optional)
- aluminum foil (optional)
- Learning-Centre Task Card: Playing With Physical Changes (2.18.1)
- sticky notes
- concept web (from lesson 12)

Engage

Provide each student with an uninflated balloon. Ask:

- How can you change the shape of the balloon?

Have students stretch and crumple up the balloons. Ask:

- How have you changed the shape of the balloon?
- Of what is the balloon made?
- Has the balloon's material changed at all?
- Can you change the balloon back to its original shape?

Now, have students blow air into the balloons and tie the end in a knot. Ask:

- Has the shape of the balloon changed?
- Can you change the balloon back to its original shape?
- Why does the balloon stay inflated? (There is air inside of the balloon.)
- What do you think will happen to the balloon if we leave it for a week?

Have students share their predictions, and then test them by leaving the balloons for a week.

After a week, have students examine their balloons. Discuss how air particles are small enough that some are actually able to slowly pass through the rubber.

NOTE: This is a valuable demonstration of the properties of matter. For more information, see "What Happened to My Balloon?" at <www.scienceshorts.com/what-happened-to-my-balloon/>.

As students examine their balloons, ask:

- Has the balloon's material changed at all during this investigation?

Introduce the guided inquiry question: **What is a physical change?**

Explore Part One

As a class, review the balloon task from the Engage activity. Discuss how it is an example of a *physical change*—a physical characteristic of the balloon was altered. The shape of the balloon changed due to more pressure on the inside.

Record the term *physical change* on chart paper. Discuss how the balloon returned to its original form when the air was released. The properties of the rubber remained the same. Ask:

- If you inflated the balloon, and then popped it, would this be a *physical change* to the balloon?
- Would the properties of the rubber be the same?

After discussion and predictions, blow up a balloon and then pop it. Gather together the pieces of the balloon. Ask:

- Did the shape of the balloon change?
- Did the properties of the balloon change?

Discuss how popping the balloon changed the shape of it, but it is still made out of the same material with which it started. This is an example of a *physical change*.

Explore Part Two

Organize the class into working groups. Explain to students that they are going to investigate physical changes in matter. To each group, distribute large paper clips, recycled scrap paper, and elastic bands. Have students manipulate each object to demonstrate physical changes.

Distribute writing paper and as a class, discuss how students might record their investigation. For example, they might make a chart, as in the example below:

Object	Before	After

Students can then record the name of each object, and draw labelled diagrams of each before and after the physical changes were made. Then have students find more objects from the classroom to change, recording these as well.

Following the investigation, ask students to co-construct a definition for *physical change*. Encourage students to use their own background knowledge and also refer to student dictionaries. Record the definition on chart paper, and have students use the new term in complete sentences to show understanding. Record these sentences on chart paper.

Formative Assessment

Observe students as they work with materials to cause physical changes. Focus specifically on their ability to perform and describe physical changes, and to discuss observations related to the properties of matter. Use the ANECDOTAL RECORD template, on page 50, to record results. Provide descriptive feedback to students about how they communicate observations about the properties of matter.

Expand

Provide students with an opportunity to explore physical changes further by posing their own inquiry questions for personalized learning. They may wish to:

- Initiate a project at the Makerspace centre, such as designing and constructing a device to crush sugar cubes.
- Explore Loose Parts related to physical changes with collections of easy-to-manipulate objects (e.g., pipe cleaners, foam, paper clips, plastic bread clips, craft sticks). Students can explore the Loose Parts to generate their own inquiry questions.
- Explore other examples of physical changes. For example, how can you change a toy car? A running shoe? A basketball? A pencil?

18

- Explore examples of physical changes that are reversible and irreversible.
- Make physical changes to various art materials (e.g., construction paper, tissue paper, foam, crêpe paper, ribbon, yarn, fabric) to create a collage or other art project.
- Conduct an investigation or experiment based on their own inquiry questions.

As students explore and select ideas to expand learning, provide support and guidance as needed, and offer access to materials and resources that will enable students to conduct their chosen investigations.

Learning Centre

At the learning centre, provide digital cameras, and various colours of modelling clay, Plasticine, or play dough, along with a copy of the Learning-Centre Task Card: Playing With Physical Changes (2.18.1):

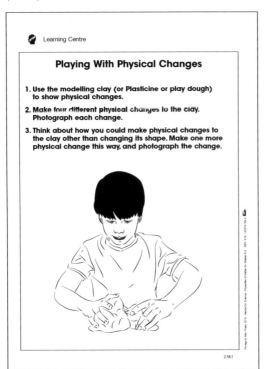

Download this template at <www.portageandmainpress.com/product/HOSMatterK2>.

Challenge students to manipulate the modelling clay, Plasticine, or play dough to demonstrate physical changes. Have students photograph the changes they make.

NOTE: Students may have ideas for other ways to demonstrate physical changes to the modelling clay (e.g., add beads or pieces of aluminum foil). Consult with students to ensure safety and appropriateness, but encourage creativity with this activity.

Embed Part One: Talking Circle

Revisit the guided inquiry question: **What is a physical change?** Have students share their knowledge and experiences, provide examples, and ask further inquiry questions.

Embed Part Two

- Add to the concept web as students learn new concepts, answer some of their own inquiry questions, and ask new inquiry questions.
- Add new terms and illustrations to the word wall. Include the words in languages other than English, such as Indigenous languages, as appropriate.
- Focus on students' use of the Core Competencies. Have students reflect on how they used one of the Core Competencies (Thinking, Communicating, or Personal and Social Skills) during the various lesson activities. Project one of the CORE COMPETENCY DISCUSSION PROMPTS templates (pages 38–42), and use it to inspire group reflection. Referring to the template, choose one or two "I Can" statements on which to focus. Students then use the "I Can" statements to provide evidence of how they demonstrated that competency. Ask

questions directly related to that competency to inspire discussion. For example:

- What did you find most interesting when learning about physical changes today? (Critical Thinking)

Have students reflect orally, encouraging participation, questions, and the sharing of evidence (see page 29 for more information on these templates).

As part of this process, students can also set goals. For example, ask:

- What would you do differently next time and why?
- How will you know if you are successful in meeting your goal?

■ To encourage self-reflection, provide prompts that students can use to cite examples of how they have used the Core Competencies in their learning. For this purpose, the CORE COMPETENCY SELF-REFLECTION FRAMES (pages 44–47) can be used throughout the learning process. There are five frames provided to address the Core Competencies: Communication, Creative Thinking, Critical Thinking, Positive Personal and Cultural Identity, and Personal Awareness and Responsibility. Conference individually with students to support self-reflection, or students may complete prompts using words and pictures.

Again, have students set goals by considering what they might do differently on future tasks and how they will know if they are successful in meeting their goal.

NOTE: Use the same prompts from these templates over time to see how thinking changes with different activities.

Enhance

- **Family Connection**: Provide students with the following sentence starter:
  - We can show a physical change at home by _____.

  Have students complete the sentence starter at home. Family members can help the student draw and write about this topic. Have students share their sentences with the class.

- Expand on the learning-centre activity and have students (with the support of an older peer or adult) make short stop-animation videos with their Plasticine creations.

- Introduce students to the water cycle to explore physical changes as water is heated or cooled. Watch videos such as:
  - "The Water Cycle" <https://www.youtube.com/watch?v=ncORPosDrjI>

  After the video, conduct demonstrations presented in the video to see water vapour and evaporation firsthand.

- Have students identify and investigate other physical changes:
  - Melt butter, and then cool it again, to see how it changes.
  - Freeze a banana, then observe as it thaws.
  - Mix soil and water into mud. Spread it on a plate to dry. Observe similarities and differences.

19 What Is a Chemical Change?

Information for Teachers

Chemical changes are evident when steel wool rusts, when apples or bananas ripen, or when a match is lit. A chemical change can happen quickly or gradually. In all cases, a chemical change is identified when the original materials are used up or altered, and new materials with unique properties and characteristics are produced.

In the case of steel wool, the starting material—steel—slowly undergoes a chemical change when oxygen from the atmosphere combines with the steel to form iron oxide (rust). This rust is unique—it has its own properties and characteristics that make it different from both steel and oxygen. This is a *chemical change*; the starting material is altered, and a new substance is produced.

Materials

- craft sticks
- white paper
- chart paper
- markers
- lighter
- kitchen tongs
- aluminum pie plate
- clear jars with lids
- student dictionaries
- stories by Indigenous authors about fire (see Explore Part Two)
- vinegar
- raw eggs
- spoons
- drawing paper
- computer/tablet with internet access
- measuring cups
- Learning-Centre Task Card: Invisible Ink! (2.19.1)
- lemon juice
- cotton swabs
- salt
- wax crayons
- hair dryer
- acidic liquids (e.g., rice or white vinegar, orange juice) (optional)
- sticky notes
- concept web (from lesson 12)

Engage

Give each student a craft stick. Have students examine their craft stick and describe its characteristics. Ask:

- Of what is the craft stick made?
- Can you cause a physical change to the craft stick?
- What would cause these changes? (pressure or force)

Have students demonstrate physical changes to their craft sticks. Ask:

- Can you change a craft stick into something other than a piece of wood?

Introduce the guided inquiry question: **What is a chemical change?**

Explore Part One

 SAFETY NOTE: The following activity uses open flame and should be conducted only as a teacher demonstration. School districts may have policies regarding flames within a school. In this case, demonstrations might be conducted outdoors. Always have a fire extinguisher or water source available when working with open flame. Remind students that they should never play with fire.

Review students' ideas about how they might change a craft stick, so it is no longer a piece of wood.

Using a pair of kitchen tongs, hold a craft stick over an aluminum pie plate. Use the lighter to begin to burn one end of the stick. While the craft stick is burning, ask:

19

- What does fire need to burn? (oxygen)
- What are the starting materials in this chemical reaction? (wood, oxygen)
- What is happening to the craft stick?
- How is the wood changed? (Smoke and ashes are produced.)

Continue to burn the craft stick while discussing students' responses. Before the entire stick burns, blow out the flame, and allow what is left of the stick to cool.

Smear the carbon and ashes from the craft stick on white paper.

Review with students that the starting materials were wood and oxygen. Adding heat (produced by igniting the lighter fluid) caused a chemical change. Ask:

- What happened to the craft stick?
- What was produced when the craft stick burned? (smoke, ash, carbon)
- Could you reverse this change?
- Is the craft stick material still wood?

Discuss that the products of this change are new and have characteristics and properties different from the starting materials. This change to the craft stick is called a *chemical change*. Record the term *chemical change* on chart paper. Ask:

- Do you think all chemical changes require heat or fire?

Have students share their ideas.

Explore Part Two

Explore Indigenous stories and knowledge about fire. Invite a local Elder or Knowledge Keeper to share stories and knowledge with the class.

NOTE: See Indigenous Perspectives and Knowledge, page 9, for guidelines for inviting Elders and Knowledge Keepers to speak to students.

Also use resources such as the following:

- *How the Robin Got Its Red Breast* by Sechelt Nation
- *The Little Hummingbird* by Michael Yahgulanaas
- *Nanabosho Steals Fire* by Joe McLellan
- *Things That Keep Us Warm* by Louise Flaherty

Discuss the role fire has played in human survival, and how that has changed over time. For example, Indigenous peoples and early European settlers relied on fire for heat and cooking. Today, most people cook with electric or gas appliances, and most homes are heated with electricity or natural gas, although many people still use wood stoves and fireplaces in their homes.

Explore Part Three

NOTE: Because working with raw eggs can be challenging in an early years classroom, this activity may be best conducted as a whole-class investigation.

Organize the class into working groups. Distribute a raw egg, vinegar, a spoon, measuring cups, and a clear jar with a lid to each group. Have each student take a turn examining and describing the raw egg. Remind students to be gentle so as to not crack or break the egg.

Next, have groups pour 250 mL of vinegar (or enough to fully immerse the egg) into their jar. Ask:

- What do you think will happen over time if the egg is placed in the vinegar?

Have students share their predictions.

Have each group use a spoon to gently place their eggs into the jar of vinegar, and then seal the jar with the lid.

▶

19

Provide students with drawing paper and have them draw a diagram of this investigation. Over the next five days, open the jars and examine the eggs. Students can record their observations using diagrams and words.

NOTE: The egg can be carefully removed from the jar in order to allow students closer examination. They may also gently touch the egg to observe the changes in the shell.

Review the investigation as a class. Ask:

- Has a chemical change taken place?

Have students share their answers and provide explanations for their ideas. Discuss their observations, and challenge them to explain why the egg shell changed. To clarify understanding, show students the following video:

- "How to Make a Naked Egg?" <https://imaginationstationtoledo.org/content/2011/04/how-to-make-a-naked-egg/>

Have students co-construct a class definition for the term *chemical change*. Encourage them to use their background knowledge to formulate ideas, and then check dictionaries for accuracy. Record definitions on chart paper along with examples written as complete sentences.

 SAFETY NOTE: Ensure students wash their hands immediately after this activity. Raw eggs can be a source of salmonella and other bacteria. For more information go to <https://www.cdc.gov/features/salmonellaeggs/index.html>.

Expand

Provide students with an opportunity to explore chemical changes further by posing their own inquiry questions for personalized learning. They may wish to:

- Initiate a project at the Makerspace centre, such as designing and constructing a juicer.
- Explore Loose Parts related to chemical changes with collections of items found in nature (e.g., leaves, twigs, nails, seeds, fruit). Students can explore the Loose Parts to generate their own inquiry questions.
- Research and explore other examples of chemical changes. For example, find out what happens when you:
  - pour vinegar on baking soda
  - place a rusty nail in cola
  - pour dish soap on a greasy plate
- Using the learning-centre activity as an inspiration, write a family member a secret message using the cotton swab dipped in lemon. Have family members "uncover" the message using a hair dryer.
- Conduct an investigation or experiment based on their own inquiry questions.

As students explore and select ideas to expand learning, provide support and guidance as needed, and offer access to materials and resources that will enable students to conduct their chosen investigations.

Learning Centre

 SAFETY NOTE: The following activity involves the use of hair dryers. Ensure the hair dryer has a low/warm setting, or consider having teachers/adults use the dryer.

At the learning centre, provide lemon juice, cotton swabs, white paper, salt, wax crayons, a hair dryer, and a copy of the Learning-Centre Task Card: Invisible Ink! (2.19.1):

19

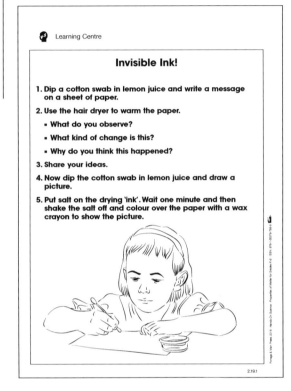

Download this template at <www.portageandmainpress.com/product/HOSMatterK2>.

Have students explore two different chemical changes, both of which allow them to write secret messages on paper using cotton swabs dipped in lemon juice—with two different ways to reveal the secret! Have students use the heat source or salt and wax crayons, then watch as the message appears.

NOTE: Lemon juice contains citric acid. Heating the lemon-juice writing causes the acid to decompose, leaving carbon on the paper—this is the message you see, and it is a non-reversible process. Once the message is visible, it stays visible. Students may also experiment with other liquids (e.g., orange or apple juice, white or rice vinegar).

Embed Part One: Talking Circle

Revisit the guided inquiry question: **What is a chemical change?** Have students share their knowledge and experiences, provide examples, and ask further inquiry questions.

Embed Part Two

- Add to the concept web as students learn new concepts, answer some of their own inquiry questions, and ask new inquiry questions.
- Add new terms and illustrations to the word wall. Include the words in languages other than English, such as Indigenous languages, as appropriate.
- Focus on students' use of the Core Competencies. Have students reflect on how they used one of the Core Competencies (Thinking, Communicating, or Personal and Social Skills) during the various lesson activities. Project one of the CORE COMPETENCY DISCUSSION PROMPTS templates (pages 38–42), and use it to inspire group reflection. Referring to the template, choose one or two "I Can" statements on which to focus. Students then use the "I Can" statements to provide evidence of how they demonstrated that competency. Ask questions directly related to that competency to inspire discussion. For example:
  - How did you show that you were an active listener today? (Communication)

Have students reflect orally, encouraging participation, questions, and the sharing of evidence (see page 29 for more information on these templates).

As part of this process, students can also set goals. For example, ask:

- What would you do differently next time and why?
- How will you know if you are successful in meeting your goal?

19

- To encourage self-reflection, provide prompts that students can use to cite examples of how they have used the Core Competencies in their learning. For this purpose, the CORE COMPETENCY SELF-REFLECTION FRAMES (pages 44–47) can be used throughout the learning process. There are five frames provided to address the Core Competencies: Communication, Creative Thinking, Critical Thinking, Positive Personal and Cultural Identity, and Personal Awareness and Responsibility. Conference individually with students to support self-reflection, or students may complete prompts using words and pictures.

    Again, have students set goals by considering what they might do differently on future tasks, and how they will know if they are successful in meeting their goal.

NOTE: Use the same prompts from these templates over time to see how thinking changes with different activities.

Enhance

- **Family Connection**: Provide students with the following sentence starter:
    - We can show a chemical change at home by _____.

    Have students complete the sentence starter at home. Family members can help the student draw and write about this topic. Have students share their sentences with the class.

    SAFETY NOTE: Ensure adult supervision is available when students explore chemical changes. Send a note home with students to encourage safe exploration of chemical changes under supervision.

20. How Does Food Preparation Depend on Physical and Chemical Changes?

Information for Teachers

Chemical and physical changes are happening all the time at school and at home. These processes are most evident in the kitchen where products such as flour, sugar, yeast, and water are combined and heated to produce foods.

In some cases, chemical changes release large amounts of energy (e.g., heat, light, sound). Baking often produces gases as well, which is how batter rises.

 SAFETY NOTE: Several activities in this lesson involve food and making treats for students to eat. Before conducting any activities that involve food, remember to consider students' medical records, and look for concerns such as allergies, diabetes, or other dietary restrictions. Also practice sanitary food preparation (e.g., washing surfaces, hands, and utensils).

Materials

- white granulated sugar
- raisins
- electric frying pan (with lid)
- chart paper
- markers
- oven mitts
- greased pan
- craft sticks
- favourite cookie recipe
- ingredients for cookies
- mixing bowls
- measuring spoons
- mixing spoons
- access to an oven
- real maple syrup
- heat source
- measuring cups
- saucepan
- cookie sheets
- snow or crushed ice
- access to freezer
- candy thermometer
- computer/tablet with internet access
- projection device (optional)
- Bannock Recipe (2.20.1)
- flour
- water
- baking powder
- shortening (animal lard)
- salt
- blueberries (optional)
- sticky notes
- concept web (from lesson 12)

Engage

 SAFETY NOTE: Only teachers should conduct tasks involving heat in the following activity. Stress safety precautions for students when working close to heat. Wear oven mitts to avoid burns.

Challenge students to identify physical or chemical changes as the changes occur in the following activity.

Have a student measure 250 mL of white granulated sugar and place it in an electric frying pan. Ask:

- What do you think will happen when we heat the sugar?
- Will this be a physical change or a chemical change?

Turn on the electric pan to medium heat, and stir gently until the sugar melts. Encourage students to observe and describe what is happening. Ask:

- What observations can you make? (The sugar is changing colour and changing into a liquid state.)

When the sugar has melted, turn off the frying pan, and stir in 125 mL of raisins. Pour the mixture onto a greased pan, and allow students to observe as it cools.

Ask:

- Has a physical change or a chemical change occurred?
- Do the sugar and the raisins remain?

Review with students the criteria for a chemical change:

- The starting materials are used up or altered.
- A completely new substance is formed with new properties.

In this investigation, both the raisins and the sugar remain (although the sugar melted and then became a solid again). No new substances have been formed. Therefore, the materials have undergone physical change, but not chemical change.

When cooled, give students an opportunity to taste and describe the treat!

Introduce the guided inquiry question: **How does food preparation depend on physical and chemical changes?**

Explore Part One

Discuss the production of maple syrup and related products investigated in lesson 14. Review the books and videos in that lesson.

Then, make maple taffy with students:

1. Place clean, fresh snow or finely crushed ice onto a cookie sheet. Pack it down, and set it outside or in the freezer, so it stays cold.
2. Pour two cups of real maple syrup into a saucepan, and bring it to a boil.
3. Put a candy thermometer in the syrup.
4. When the syrup reaches 112°C, take it off the heat and immediately drizzle it in several lines over the packed snow in the cookie sheet.
5. Let the syrup cool for just a minute or two. Have each student press a craft stick into the taffy, then roll it until the end of the stick is covered in a thick piece of candy—eat and enjoy!

Discuss the changes that occurred to the maple syrup and the effects of both heating and cooling.

Explore Part Two

Have students suggest favourite cookie recipes. This is an excellent opportunity for family involvement to gather recipes and also to come to the class to make favourite cookie recipes.

Select one recipe to make as a class. Record the recipe on chart paper, or project it for the class to see.

NOTE: To support students as they make the cookies, consider having older peers or volunteers help groups of students.

Display the cookie recipe. Review the ingredients, equipment, and procedures for making the cookies.

Organize the class into working groups. Provide each group with the cookie ingredients, mixing bowls, measuring cups and spoons, mixing spoons, and cookie sheets.

Guide students through the process of making the cookies. Have them:

1. Examine each ingredient used in the recipe and describe its characteristics.
2. Mix the cookie dough.
3. Describe the characteristics of the cookie dough.
4. Predict what will happen as the cookies bake. (How will the dough change?)
5. Bake the cookies.

Allow the cookies to cool. Before eating them, focus students' attention on the finished product. Ask:

- In what ways have we changed the original ingredients (both chemically and physically)?
- Are these changes in the ingredients reversible or nonreversible?
- What role did heat play in this activity?

To explain the chemical reactions that occur while baking cookies, show students the following video:

- "The chemistry of cookies—Stephanie Warren" <https://www.youtube.com/watch?v=n6wpNhyreDE>

Formative Assessment

Observe students as they make cookies. Focus specifically on their ability to follow directions and measure accurately. Use the ANECDOTAL RECORD template, on page 50, to record results. Provide descriptive feedback to students about how they follow directions, measure accurately, and describe the changes in the cookies.

Explore Part Three

Invite a local Elder, Knowledge Keeper, or other Indigenous community member into the classroom to share a recipe with students and discuss food preparation.

NOTE: See Indigenous Perspectives and Knowledge, page 9, for guidelines for inviting Elders and Knowledge Keepers to speak to students.

The First Nations Health Authority also provides "Traditional Food Fact Sheets" that include several recipes and other information that may be useful for this activity: <www.fnhc.ca/pdf/Traditional_Food_Facts_Sheets.pdf>.

Have students make other recipes such as bannock (2.20.1):

Bannock

Ingredients
- 1000 mL (4 cups) flour
- 500 mL (2 cups) water
- 60 mL (4 tbsp) baking powder
- 60 mL (4 tbsp) shortening (animal lard), room temperature
- 5 mL (1 tsp) salt
- blueberries (optional)
- raisins (optional)

Instructions
1. Stir flour, baking powder, and salt together thoroughly.
2. Add shortening to the flour mixture until small lumps are formed in the flour.
3. Make a crater in the flour mixture, and pour in water, making a lake.
4. Add blueberries or raisins, if desired, and mix gently until dough is formed.
5. Pat dough into a greased 9 x 12 inch pan, and bake at 350° F (180° C) for about an hour or until golden brown.

2.20.1

Download this template at <www.portageandmainpress.com/product/HOSMatterK2>.

Connect this activity with books about food preparation by Indigenous authors, such as:

- *I Can't Have Bannock, but the Beaver Has a Dam* by Bernelda Wheeler
- *Awâsis and the World-Famous Bannock* by Dallas Hunt

Expand

Provide students with an opportunity to further explore physical and chemical changes in cooking by posing their own inquiry questions for personalized learning. They may wish to:

- Initiate a project at the Makerspace centre, such as designing and constructing a unique cookie cutter.

▶

- Explore Loose Parts related to chemical changes with collections of cooking and baking utensils. Students can explore the Loose Parts to generate their own inquiry questions.
- Collect family recipes and make a recipe book.
- Demonstrate cooking a favourite recipe.
- Video record a cooking show with family members.
- Research and explore other examples of physical and chemical changes in food preparation. For example:
  - make homemade ice cream or ice pops
  - collect edible wild foods in the local area (under supervision)
- Conduct an investigation or experiment based on their own inquiry questions.

As students explore and select ideas to expand learning, provide support and guidance as needed, and offer access to materials and resources that will enable students to conduct their chosen investigations.

Embed Part One: Talking Circle

Revisit the guided inquiry question: **How does food preparation depend on physical and chemical changes?** Have students share their knowledge and experiences, provide examples, and ask further inquiry questions.

Embed Part Two

- Add to the concept web as students learn new concepts, answer some of their own inquiry questions, and ask new inquiry questions.
- Add new terms and illustrations to the word wall. Include the words in languages other than English, such as Indigenous languages, as appropriate.

- Focus on students' use of the Core Competencies. Have students reflect on how they used one of the Core Competencies (Thinking, Communicating, or Personal and Social Skills) during the various lesson activities. Project one of the CORE COMPETENCY DISCUSSION PROMPTS templates (pages 38–42), and use it to inspire group reflection. Referring to the template, choose one or two "I Can" statements on which to focus. Students then use the "I Can" statements to provide evidence of how they demonstrated that competency. Ask questions directly related to that competency to inspire discussion. For example:
  - How did you share your learning today? (Communication)

  Have students reflect orally, encouraging participation, questions, and the sharing of evidence (see page 29 for more information on these templates).

  As part of this process, students can also set goals. For example, ask:
  - What would you do differently next time and why?
  - How will you know if you are successful in meeting your goal?

- To encourage self-reflection, provide prompts that students can use to cite examples of how they have used the Core Competencies in their learning. For this purpose, the CORE COMPETENCY SELF-REFLECTION FRAMES (pages 44–47) can be used throughout the learning process. There are five frames provided to address the Core Competencies: Communication, Creative Thinking, Critical Thinking, Positive Personal and Cultural Identity, and Personal Awareness and Responsibility. Conference individually with students to support self-reflection, or students may complete prompts using words and pictures.

Again, have students set goals by considering what they might do differently on future tasks, and how they will know if they are successful in meeting their goal.

NOTE: Use the same prompts from these templates over time to see how thinking changes with different activities.

Enhance

- **Family Connection**: Provide students with the following sentence starter:
    - We can show physical and chemical changes at home by preparing food such as _____.

    Have students complete the sentence starter at home. Family members can help the student draw and write about this topic. Have students share their sentences with the class.

- Popping popcorn is another opportunity to observe changes in substances. If you watch closely as kernels pop, you will see a little puff of gas (steam). Challenge students to explore why this happens.

- Demonstrate frying an egg for students to observe the chemical changes. The heat breaks down proteins in the egg, and the clear part of the egg turns white (while the yolk remains yellow).

- Investigate how the cooling process is used to make various foods (e.g., flavoured gelatin dessert, popped rice treats, snow cones, ice cream). Discuss whether each example demonstrates a chemical or a physical change.

- Have students brainstorm the steps involved in making a healthy meal using the Canada Food Guide. Then have them identify the physical and chemical changes that occur. Have groups construct t-charts to show their meals, such as the following example:

Physical Changes	Chemical Changes
chopping salad veggies	baking pizza crust

- Show students the film by the National Film Board "Zea" <https://www.nfb.ca/film/zea_en/> without telling them what they are observing. The video shows amazing transformation through cooking. Have students watch and share ideas about what is happening with a partner. The end is a great surprise!

21 | Inquiry Project: What More Do We Want to Know About the Properties of Matter?

Materials

- herringbone chart from lessons 3–11
- concept web from lessons 12–20
- sticky notes
- word wall
- chart paper
- markers
- variety of objects and materials from previous lessons (e.g., collections of natural objects such as stones, leaves, seeds, twigs; objects made of different materials such as plastic, metal, fabric, wood, glass; containers of liquids, balloons filled with air)
- bins or basins for holding collections (one for each working group)
- digital camera*

*NOTE: Use a digital camera to photograph students participating in the lesson's activities and collect evidence of learning for students' portfolios.

Engage

Begin the lesson with the class sitting in a circle on the carpet. In the centre of the circle, have a variety of objects and materials that were used throughout the module (e.g., collections of natural objects such as stones, leaves, seeds, twigs; objects made of different materials such as plastic, metal, fabric, wood, glass; containers of liquids, balloons filled with air).

Review with the class how the different objects were used and what each one taught the class about the properties of matter. Refer to the herringbone chart, the concept web, and the word wall to expand discussion and encourage the sharing of ideas.

Introduce the guided inquiry question: **What more do we want to know about the properties of matter?**

Explore Part One

Explain to students that they will create their own collections of objects or materials. These might be compared to the discovery bins of Loose Parts, so students have an understanding of how a collection might look. As a class, brainstorm a list of ideas for collections that students might consider. For example:

- local rocks, seeds, leaves, feathers, twigs
- objects made of plastic, metal, fabric, wood, glass, paper
- objects made of more than one material
- liquids (collected in pill bottles or baby food jars)
- objects that float in water
- objects that sink in water
- objects that attract to a magnet
- objects that do not absorb liquids easily
- objects that absorb liquids easily
- objects that melt easily*
- objects used for cooking*
- objects that are flexible/pliable/mendable

 ***SAFETY NOTE:** These collections can be tested with adult supervision.

Record students' ideas on chart paper.

Organize the class into pairs or working groups, based on interest in specific collections. Students may also choose to work independently. Give students time to discuss ideas for their collections.

Provide each student or group with a bin for holding their collection. Give them time to gather objects for their collection from the classroom, from home, and from the community (with supervision). Collaborate with students to determine a date to present their completed collections to the class, as well as the number of objects (minimum/maximum) they should collect.

Explore Part Two

When students/groups have completed their collection, provide time for them to explore and discuss the items independently before their formal presentations. Encourage them to:

- identify each object
- describe characteristics (e.g., texture, colour, shape, size, solid/liquid) of each object
- describe how the objects in their collection are the same
- identify differences in the objects in the collection

Record this criteria on chart paper and post it where students can see it while preparing for their presentations.

Explore Part Three

Have each student/group present their collection to the class. Again, encourage them use the criteria listed in Explore Part Two.

When all collections have been presented, provide time for students to explore each collection. Spread out the bins on tables around the classroom and have students work in groups to examine and discuss each collection.

Expand

Provide students with an opportunity to explore collections further by posing their own inquiry questions for personalized learning. They may wish to:

- Initiate a project at the Makerspace centre, such as designing and constructing a display case for their collection.
- Explore Loose Parts related to properties of matter with collections of objects used throughout the module, as well as other collections (e.g., buttons, bottle caps, marker caps). Students can explore the Loose Parts to generate their own inquiry questions.
- Create another collection based on different properties.
- Interview community or family members who have collections (e.g., rocks, stamps, baseball cards).
- Conduct an investigation or experiment based on their own inquiry questions.

As students explore and select ideas to expand learning, provide support and guidance as needed, and offer access to materials and resources that will enable students to conduct their chosen investigations.

Embed Part One: Talking Circle

Revisit the guided inquiry question: **What more do we want to know about the properties of matter?** Have students share their knowledge and experiences, and provide examples to consolidate learning.

Embed Part Two

- Add to the concept web as students learn new concepts, answer some of their own inquiry questions, and ask new inquiry questions.
- Add new terms and illustrations to the word wall. Include the words in languages other than English, such as Indigenous languages, as appropriate.
- Focus on students' use of the Core Competencies. Have students reflect on how they used one of the Core Competencies (Thinking, Communicating, or Personal and Social Skills) during the various lesson activities. Project one of the CORE COMPETENCY DISCUSSION PROMPTS templates (pages 38–42), and use it to inspire group reflection. Referring to the template, choose one or two "I Can" statements on which to focus. Students then use the "I Can" statements to provide evidence of how they demonstrated that competency. Ask

21

questions directly related to that competency to inspire discussion. For example:

- How did you make your ideas work on your inquiry project? (Creative Thinking)

Have students reflect orally, encouraging participation, questions, and the sharing of evidence (see page 29 for more information on these templates).

As part of this process, students can also set goals. For example, ask:

- What would you do differently next time and why?
- How will you know if you are successful in meeting your goal?

- To encourage self-reflection, provide prompts that students can use to cite examples of how they have used the Core Competencies in their learning. For this purpose, the CORE COMPETENCY SELF-REFLECTION FRAMES (pages 44–47) can be used throughout the learning process. There are five frames provided to address the Core Competencies: Communication, Creative Thinking, Critical Thinking, Positive Personal and Cultural Identity, and Personal Awareness and Responsibility. Conference individually with students to support self-reflection, or students may complete prompts using words and pictures.

Again, have students set goals by considering what they might do differently on future tasks, and how they will know if they are successful in meeting their goal.

NOTE: Use the same prompts from these templates over time to see how thinking changes with different activities.

Module Assessment Summary

- Collect student work in a portfolio (see The *Hands-On Science* Assessment Plan, page 29), so students can examine and discuss these artifacts of learning during a student/teacher conference. This collection may include photographs they have taken, drawings, place-based journals, and other evidence of learning. This will allow students to recall specific activities and learning experiences and to reflect on their use of the Core Competencies throughout the module.

- Have students take home a copy of the FAMILY AND COMMUNITY CONNECTIONS: ASSESSING TOGETHER template on page 57. Have them complete the template with a family or community member (with permission) to reflect on their learning about the properties of matter.

- Have students focus on the CORE COMPETENCY STUDENT REFLECTIONS MODULE SUMMARY template, on page 48, to reflect on their use of the Core Competencies throughout the module. Students' reflections are recorded in the rectangle on the template (using pictures and text). The student then considers next steps in learning as related to that particular Core Competency. These reflections are recorded in the arrow in the template, again, using words and drawings.

- Review all assessment templates completed throughout the module. This includes all documentation for student self-assessment, formative assessment, and summative assessment. This will provide a more comprehensive picture of student progress as related to the Big Ideas, Core Competencies, Curricular Competencies, and Content of the module.

Appendix: Image Banks

Images appearing in the appendix are thumbnails from the Image Banks referenced in the lessons. Corresponding full-page, high-resolution images can be printed or projected for the related lessons, and are found on the Portage & Main Press website at: <www.portageandmainpress.com/product/HOSMATTERK2/>. Use the password **OBJECTSANDMATERIALS** to access the download for free. This link and password can also be used to access the reproducible templates for this module.

Lesson 6: Why are Some Materials Better Than Others for Certain Jobs?
Tools of First Peoples in British Columbia

1. Quwutsun', Coast Salish Canoe Bailer
Materials: cedar bark, wood

2. Coast Salish Cod Lure
Materials: wood, cherry bark, metal

3. Saanich, Coast Salish Loom
Materials: wood, metal

4. Haida Carving Knife
Materials: wood, steel, cedar bark, lacquer

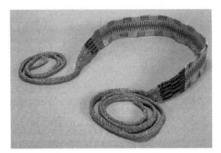

5. Sto:lo, Coast Salish Tumpline
Materials: burlap, wool, cotton, dye

Image Credits:

1 – Canoe Bailer Object ID #A8071, photographed by Derek Tan. Courtesy of UBC Museum of Anthropology, Vancouver, Canada.

2 – Cod Lure Object ID #Nbz688 a-c, photographed by Derek Tan. Courtesy of UBC Museum of Anthropology, Vancouver, Canada.

3 – Loom Object ID #A8199, photographed by Jessica Bushey. Courtesy of UBC Museum of Anthropology, Vancouver, Canada.

4 – sdaaxuunang.uu (Knife) Object ID #Nb1.475, photographed by Kyla Bailey. Courtesy of UBC Museum of Anthropology, Vancouver, Canada.

5 – q'si:ltel (Tumpline) Object ID #A8757, photographed by Derek Tan. Courtesy of UBC Museum of Anthropology, Vancouver, Canada.

Lesson 7: How Can Different Materials Be Used to Construct Objects?
Canoes

1. Algonquin Bark Canoe
Materials: birchbark, spruce root, pitch, cedar

2. Inuit Umiak
Materials: sealskin, sinew, assorted wood

3. Kwakwaka'wakw Dugout Canoe
Materials: red cedar

176

4. Gwitch'in Bark Canoe

Materials: birchbark, tree roots, assorted wood, pitch, glass beads

5. Kalaallit Hunting Kayak

Materials: sealskin, sinew, assorted wood

6. Salish Clam Canoe

Materials: red cedar

7. Squamish Canoe

Materials: red cedar

8. Haida Canoe

Materials: red cedar

Image Credits:

1 – Algonquin Bark Canoe. Courtesy of the Canadian Canoe Museum and Michael Cullen.

2 – Umiak. Courtesy of the Canadian Canoe Museum and Michael Cullen.

3 – Dugout Canoe. Courtesy of the Canadian Canoe Museum and Michael Cullen.

4 – Gwitch'in bark canoe. Courtesy of the Canadian Canoe Museum and Michael Cullen.

5 – Western Greenland Hunting Kayak. Courtesy of the Canadian Canoe Museum and Michael Cullen.

6 – Salish clam canoe. Courtesy of the Canadian Canoe Museum and Michael Cullen.

7 – Squamish canoe. Courtesy of the Canadian Canoe Museum and Michael Cullen.

8 – Haida canoe. Courtesy of the Canadian Canoe Museum and Michael Cullen.

Lesson 9: Why Is It Important to Choose the Right Materials for the Job?
Indigenous Homes

1. The Kwakwaka'wakw Mungo Martin House

2. Reconstructed Dakelh Pit House

3. Reconstructed Dakelh Pit House

4. 'Namgis Traditional Big House

5. Haida Heritage Centre

6. Eastern Woodlands Birchbark Wigwam

Image Credits:

1 – 4 Thunderbird Park Lodge House, Victoria by Lisa Andres. Used under CC by 2.0 licence.

2 – FNST 161: Building a Pit House Image 10 of 10 by the First Nations Studies Department, the University of Northern British Columbia.

3 – FNST 161: Building a Pit House Image 4 of 10 by the First Nations Studies Department, the University of Northern British Columbia.

4 – Namgis Big House by David Stanley. Used under CC by 2.0 licence.

5 – Haida Gwaii by Gingerbeer4. Used under CC0 by 1.0 licence.

6 – Ottawa Sept 17 2006 028 by Adam Kahtava. Used under CC by 2.0 licence.

Lesson 16: How Can We Combine Solids and Liquids to Make Useful Products?
First Peoples Clothing

1. Quwutsun', Coast Salish Jacket
Materials: skin, hair, glass, plastic, metal

2. Haida Chilkat Tunic
Materials: mountain goat wool, yellow cedar bark, sea otter skin, natural dye, cotton

3. Nisga'a Chilkat Robe
Materials: mountain goat wool, cotton, linen, jute, hemlock bark, wolf moss dye, cedar bark, otter skin

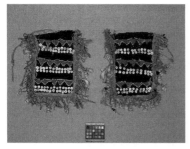
4. Gitxsan Leggings
Materials: wool, puffin beak, animal skin, glass, shell

5. Mamalilikala or Kwakwaka'wakw Headdress
Materials: wood, ermine skin, cotton, abalone shell, sea lion whisker, silver alloy metal, glass

6. Kaska Dena or Tahltan Beaded Panel
Materials: cotton, silk, glass, brass

Image Credits:

1 – Jacket Object ID #1057/3, photographed by Derek Tan. Courtesy of UBC Museum of Anthropology, Vancouver, Canada.
2 – Chilkat Tunic Object ID# A7080, photographed by Kyla Bailey. Courtesy of UBC Museum of Anthropology, Vancouver, Canada.
3 – gwiis halayt (Chilkat Robe) Object ID # A7079, photographed by Tim Bonham. Courtesy of UBC Museum of Anthropology, Vancouver, Canada.
4 – silk em séé (Leggings) Object ID #A7965 a-b, photographed by Jessica Bushey. Courtesy of UBC Museum of Anthropology, Vancouver, Canada.
5 – yaxwi'we' (Headdress) Object ID #A4173, photographed by Jessica Bushey. Courtesy of UBC Museum of Anthropology, Vancouver, Canada.
6 – Beaded Panel Object ID #3203/3, photographed by Alina Ilyasova. Courtesy of UBC Museum of Anthropology, Vancouver, Canada.

Creative Commons Licences

CC BY 2.0: Attribution 2.0 Generic <https://creativecommons.org/licences/by/2.0/>
CC BY-SA 2.0: Attribution-ShareAlike 2.0 Generic <https://creativecommons.org/licenses/by-sa/2.0/>
CC BY 4.0: Attribution 4.0 International <https://creativecommons.org/licences/by/4.0/>
Public Domain Mark 1.0: <https://creativecommons.org/publicdomain/mark/1.0/>
CC0 1.0 Universal: <https://creativecommons.org/publicdomain/zero/1.0/>

About the Contributors

Jennifer Lawson, PhD, is the originator and senior author of the Hands-On series in all subject areas. Jennifer is a former classroom teacher, resource/special education teacher, consultant, and principal. She continues to develop new Hands-On projects, and also serves as a school trustee for the St. James-Assiniboia School Division in Winnipeg, Manitoba.

Rosalind Poon has been a science teacher and Teacher Consultant for Assessment and Literacy with the Richmond School District for the past 18 years. In her current role, she works with school teams to plan and implement various aspects of the curriculum by collaborating with teams in professional inquiry groups on topics such as descriptive feedback, inquiry, assessment, and differentiation. Her passions include her family, dragon boating, cooking with the Instant Pot and making sure that all students have access to great hands-on science experiences.

Deidre Sagert specializes in early years education, and is currently working as the Early Years Support Teacher for the St. James-Assiniboia School Division. She brings 20 years of experience to her current role where she mentors early years teachers in incorporating play-based learning and inquiry into all subject areas. She is passionate about ensuring all students have access to a stimulating environment where they are engaged in hands-on experiences and authentic learning. She enjoys spending time with her family in nature for rejuvenation and inspiration.

Melanie Nelson is from the In-SHUCK-ch and Stó:lō Nations, and has experience teaching kindergarten through grade 12, as well as adults in the Lower Mainland of British Columbia. She has taught in mainstream, adapted, modified, and alternate settings, at the classroom, whole school, and district levels. Trained as an educator in science, Melanie approaches Western science through an Indigenous worldview and with Indigenous ways of knowing. Her Master of Arts thesis explored the experience of Indigenous parents who have a child identified as having special needs in school, and she is currently completing a Doctor of Philosophy in School Psychology at the University of British Columbia.

Lisa Schwartz has been a Teacher Consultant for Assessment and Literacy with the Richmond School District for the past six years. As a consultant, Lisa facilitates professional learning with small groups and school staffs on topics such as the redesigned curriculum, Core Competencies, differentiation, inquiry, and assessment. She also works side by side with teachers co-planning, co-teaching and providing demonstration lessons to highlight quality, research-based instruction that supports all learners. Lisa is passionate about engagement, joyful learning, and success for all students.